The Control of the Past

Herbert Butterfield and the Pitfalls of Official History

Patrick Salmon

LONDON
INSTITUTE OF HISTORICAL RESEARCH

Published by

UNIVERSITY OF LONDON
SCHOOL OF ADVANCED STUDY
INSTITUTE OF HISTORICAL RESEARCH
Senate House, Malet Street, London WC1E 7HU

ISBNs
978-1-914477-19-5 (paperback)
978-1-914477-22-5 (.epub)
978-1-914477-20-1 (.mobi)
978-1-914477-21-8 (.pdf)

DOI
10.14296/202112.9781914477218

Contents

About the author		v
Acknowledgements		vii
Prologue		ix
1.	'One of his most violent essays'	1
2.	Butterfield and official history	25
3.	Official history then and now	45
4.	Why bother with Butterfield?	65

Appendix I
Herbert Butterfield on official history:
Correspondence with the Rev A.W. Blaxall,
April–May 1952   69

Appendix II
Cabinet Office official histories of the
Second World War   75

Appendix III
Cabinet Office peacetime official histories   79

Appendix IV
Foreign Office documentary series   83

Bibliography   89
Index   99

About the author

PATRICK SALMON is Chief Historian at the Foreign, Commonwealth and Development Office. He was formerly Professor of International History at the University of Newcastle upon Tyne. He is a Fellow of the Royal Historical Society and a Foreign Member of the Norwegian Academy of Science and Letters. His publications include *Scandinavia and the Great Powers 1890–1940* (1997), *Deadlock and Diversion: Scandinavia in British Strategy during the Twilight War 1939–1940* (2012) and several volumes in the series *Documents on British Policy Overseas* (DBPO), including *German Unification, 1989–1990* (2009), *The Challenge of Apartheid: UK–South African Relations, 1985–1986* (2017) and *The Unwinding of Apartheid: UK–South African Relations, 1986–1990* (2019).

Acknowledgements

I am grateful to the staff of the Manuscripts Room at Cambridge University Library for access to the Butterfield papers in their care, to Sophia Lambert for the loan of Margaret Lambert's papers, and to Chris Calladine for sharing his memories of Herbert Butterfield. Gill Bennett, Michael Bentley, Philip Carter, Jim Daly, Keith Hamilton, David Hayton, Sara Hiorns, Michael Kennedy, Colin Kidd and Denis Smyth have all made valuable comments on earlier versions of this book.

I also wish to thank Philip Carter and Philip Murphy for accepting this book for inclusion in the IHR Shorts series, and Robert Davies, Lauren De'Ath and Jamie Bowman for their help in preparing it for publication.

Although I am an employee of HM Government, none of what I have written should be taken as an expression of official policy.

All hyperlinks were checked on 11 April 2021.

Prologue

Nearly fifty years ago, when I was an undergraduate at Peterhouse, Cambridge, I would occasionally see the small figure of the former Master of the College, Sir Herbert Butterfield, walking across the grass of Old Court. The thought of accosting him would never have crossed my mind, and I remained just as diffident after I became a research student in 1974. Yet if I had spoken to Sir Herbert I might have learned something of value, and I knew that at the time. For I had started to study the complex and unedifying history of British plans for military action in Scandinavia in 1939–40. My friend Denis Smyth (now emeritus professor at the University of Toronto) *had* spoken to Sir Herbert, who had recalled the time when he was visited during the war by the eminent historian and former Foreign Minister of Norway Professor Halvdan Koht. I know now that the visit took place in February 1941, just before Koht, recently deposed as Foreign Minister in the Norwegian government in exile, went into a second exile in the United States.[1] Koht told Butterfield, so Denis reported, that when Germany invaded Norway in April 1940, Britain had been on the verge of doing the same thing. Of course, I already knew that Britain had evolved some sort of plan for military action in Norway at that time; nevertheless it was striking to have the case stated so bluntly, and by such a significant source. I never followed it up.

The connection between Koht and Butterfield was Harold Temperley, Butterfield's doctoral supervisor and Koht's friend and collaborator in the International Committee of Historical Sciences, who had died prematurely in July 1939, just over a year after his (Temperley's) election as Master of Peterhouse. The connection between Denis Smyth and Butterfield was Desmond Williams, Professor of Modern History at University College Dublin. Despite the ostensible differences in their personalities, Butterfield's friendship with this 'gifted, charming, drunken, aggressive, unstable, unreliable Irishman' (in the words of Butterfield's latest biographer) was one of the closest and most important of his life.[2] Williams was an inspiring if exasperating teacher who sent generations of students to pursue their PhD studies at Peterhouse, usually (and wisely) under the supervision of

[1] Åsmund Svendsen, *Halvdan Koht. Veien mot framtiden. En biografi* (Oslo, 2013), p. 365.
[2] Michael Bentley, *The Life and Thought of Herbert Butterfield: History, Science and God* (Cambridge, 2011), p. 163.

members of other colleges (both Denis and I were supervised by Professor Harry Hinsley of St John's). Desmond visited Peterhouse frequently and would hold court in the small guest bedroom behind the porter's lodge. I got to know him quite well and can testify to his brilliance and charm, as well as his personal kindness: I had forgotten until recently that it was his reference that secured me a place at the Institut für Europäische Geschichte in Mainz (another Butterfield/Williams connection) in 1977. I was not exposed to Desmond's less admirable qualities.

Although Butterfield remained a remote and, to me, intimidating figure (already failing, he was to die in 1979), I dutifully read several of his works. I already knew his most famous and most accessible book, *The Whig Interpretation of History* (1931); I now sought insights in the dense narrative of *The Peace Tactics of Napoleon, 1806–1809*, Butterfield's PhD thesis published in 1929, and in his 1954 Wiles Lectures, published in 1955 as *Man on His Past*. Around this time I also discovered a shabby copy of *History and Human Relations*, a collection of essays published in 1951. One chapter, 'Official history: Its pitfalls and criteria', spoke directly to me as a new student of modern British history, tackling official papers and publications for the first time. I was captivated by Butterfield's subversiveness: by his hostility towards, and suspicion of, what officialdom tells us and, above all, what it does not want us to know. I can still see the passages I marked with pencil in the margin, including some that have become famous: 'It may be necessary that official history should be produced. It is equally necessary that it should be subjected to unremitting scrutiny'; 'I do not personally believe that there is a government in Europe which wants the public to know all the truth.'[3] And, as a student trying to understand conflict between Britain and Germany, it came as a revelation when Butterfield described that conflict as a mere thirty-year interlude in the longer confrontation between Britain and Russia.

Many years later, I became an official historian myself: the direct successor of Temperley and others as an editor of British diplomatic documents. For a long time after that, I was too busy to dwell on the implications of turning from poacher to gamekeeper; but, looking for something to keep me occupied during a period of convalescence, I returned to Butterfield. Living in Cambridge, I checked the Butterfield papers at the University Library and found a file entitled 'Official History'. It seemed promising, and it was. I later discovered much more, including his extensive correspondence with Desmond Williams. All this material, of course, was well known to

---

[3] Herbert Butterfield, 'Official history: Its pitfalls and criteria', in *History and Human Relations* (London, 1951), pp. 182–224 (quoted from pp. 185–6).

Butterfield's biographers and the growing body of Butterfield scholars.[4] I nevertheless became intrigued by the way in which his views on official history seemed to have evolved from early misgivings, at the time when he was close to Harold Temperley, to fierce suspicion under the influence of his new friend Desmond Williams. Untangling that relationship became a detective story of the kind that Butterfield relished, eventually bumping up against one of the more tenacious conspiracy theories of the post-war era: what the Duke of Windsor might or might not have been up to in Spain and Portugal in the summer of 1940.

My version of that story occupies the first chapter of this book. But I also wanted to discover what Butterfield actually thought and wrote about official history. That meant, on the one hand, looking at his correspondence with some of the leading historians of his day, official and unofficial – including E.L. Woodward, W.N. Medlicott and A.J.P. Taylor – and, on the other, analysing what he wrote in the two versions of his chapter: the original version published in the Irish journal *Studies* in 1949[5] and the revised version that appeared two years later.[6] That task takes up my second chapter. I then examine what happened to official history in the decades after Butterfield published his article, focusing on the wartime and peacetime narrative histories and the British and German documentary series. In the final chapter I end with some reflections on what Butterfield's admonitions might mean for official history today. Official history as it existed for much of the twentieth century – with the inauguration of the Cabinet Office's official history series in 1908 and the Foreign Office's publication of diplomatic documents on the origins of the war in 1924 – may be under threat. But governments have recently been given many reminders that history matters; and it is Butterfield above all who reminds us that we need to remain vigilant in monitoring how they respond to the challenge.

---

[4] See, in addition to Michael Bentley, C.T. McIntire, *Herbert Butterfield: Historian as Dissenter* (New Haven and London, 2004).

[5] Herbert Butterfield, 'Official history: Its pitfalls and its criteria', *Studies: An Irish Quarterly Review*, xxxviii (June 1949), 129–44.

[6] The two versions are hereafter cited as *Studies* and *Human Relations*: together if the quotation is identical, or nearly so; separately if the quotation appears only in one version.

1. 'One of his most violent essays'

The year 1949 was Herbert Butterfield's *annus mirabilis*. In that year – indeed in a single month – he published no fewer than three books. *George III, Lord North and the People*, *Christianity and History* and *The Origins of Modern Science 1300–1800* all appeared in October 1949. Only *George III* resembled anything like a conventional historical monograph.[1] The other two were ground-breaking. *Christianity and History*, based on a series of lectures given in Cambridge in the autumn of 1948 and repeated over the BBC the following Easter, answered to the widely felt need for spiritual and historical explanation at a time of recovery from war and incipient cold war, and sold 30,000 copies. *The Origins of Modern Science*, based on lectures given in Cambridge earlier in 1948, almost single-handedly established the history of science as a new scholarly discipline. For Butterfield, aged forty-nine, Methodist lay preacher, Fellow of Peterhouse, Cambridge, since 1923 and Professor of Modern History at Cambridge since 1944, these two books marked his emergence as a figure of major intellectual importance both nationally and internationally. They also represented the culmination of four years of almost unremitting creativity and hard work. It was not surprising that, as Michael Bentley writes, 'By the autumn of 1949 Butterfield was utterly wrecked with exhaustion.'[2] Fortunately for his health and his state of mind, he was then to embark on what he was to look back on as 'the best moment of his academic life': a long-anticipated sabbatical term at the Princeton Institute for Advanced Study.[3]

Yet these books did not mark the limit of Butterfield's activity in the years 1948–9. In the course of 1949 alone, he published his six BBC lectures in the *Listener*; further articles on Christianity and history and the history of science; and an article on Charles James Fox in the *Cambridge Historical Journal*.[4] And in June 1949 an article appeared in the Irish journal *Studies*, which reflected a quite different preoccupation. 'Official history: Its pitfalls and its criteria' is better known in the version that was included, considerably revised and extended, in a collection of Butterfield's essays,

---

[1] Although it was also the first salvo in his war of attrition against Lewis Namier: see David Hayton, *Conservative Revolutionary: The Lives of Lewis Namier* (Manchester, 2019), pp. 366–75.

[2] Bentley, *Butterfield*, p. 223.

[3] Ibid., p. 251.

[4] As listed in McIntire, *Butterfield*, pp. 475–6.

History and Human Relations, published in 1951; and it is this second version that has attracted attention over the years on the part of both Butterfield specialists and those interested in official history as scholars, practitioners or critics. Butterfield's article represents perhaps the most critical judgement on official history written by any British historian since the Second World War. Michael Bentley describes it as 'one of his most violent essays',[5] and it contains some of his most striking and most frequently quoted aphorisms.[6] However, such shafts of brilliance are embedded in Butterfield's typically contorted, elliptical and sometimes surprisingly apologetic prose; and it is difficult to discern in the article a sustained or coherent argument as opposed to a succession of assertions, some well founded, others of doubtful provenance. It is all very different from A.J.P. Taylor, the historian who most closely resembles Butterfield in his scepticism towards official history. Taylor delighted in expressing his views on the defective editing of British and German diplomatic documents of the inter-war period, pungently, repetitively and in the most public places: his favoured outlets were the *Times Literary Supplement* and the *Manchester Guardian*.[7] Publishing in an Irish journal and a modest volume of essays, Butterfield was less forthright, less willing to cause offence or to lose friends; yet at his best he achieved insights that Taylor never matched.

Some readers of his article have welcomed Butterfield's vigilance in keeping editors of diplomatic documents up to the mark, foremost among them the late Keith Wilson, perhaps the historian who comes closest to being Butterfield's spiritual heir in this respect.[8] Others have deplored his apparent implication that Britain should have made peace with Nazi Germany in order to let Germany and Russia fight each other to destruction.[9] Richard Aldrich has even suggested that Butterfield was making 'a comment on

[5] Michael Bentley, 'Herbert Butterfield and the ethics of historiography', *History and Theory*, xliv (Feb. 2005), 55–71 (p. 59).

[6] See the examples quoted in note 3 above (from *Studies*, p. 130; *Human Relations*, pp. 185–6).

[7] Taylor's reviews are helpfully collected in *Struggles for Supremacy: Diplomatic Essays by A.J.P. Taylor*, ed. Chris Wrigley (Aldershot, 2000).

[8] Keith Wilson, 'Introduction: Governments, historians, and "historical engineering"', in *Forging the Collective Memory: Governments and International Relations Through Two World Wars*, ed. Wilson (Providence, RI, and London, 1996), pp. 1–27. For earlier responses, see R.F.V. Heuston, review of *War Crimes Trials*, vols 4 and 5 (*The Hadamar and Natzweiler Trials*) and *Law Reports of Trials of War Criminals*, vols 10–13, *International Law Quarterly*, iii (Apr. 1950), 307–9 (p. 309); Frank Spencer, 'The publication of British and German diplomatic documents for the period of the inter-war years', *History*, xlvii (1962), 254–86 (p. 258).

[9] Paul Sharp, 'Herbert Butterfield, the English school and the civilizing virtues of diplomacy', *International Affairs*, lxxix (Jul. 2003), 855–78 (p. 868).

Ultra as the "missing dimension" of the official histories the war'.[10] This last claim is wide of the mark. I believe that Butterfield's preoccupations were more old-fashioned and had more to do with traditional despatches and telegrams than with signals intelligence and codebreaking (although, as it happens, Bletchley Park and its environs do play a part in the story).

For in accepting an invitation from 'the Historical Society of University College, Dublin',[11] to give a paper on 'contemporary history' on 14 December 1948 – the paper that became the basis of his official history article[12] – Butterfield was returning to a subject that had preoccupied him almost since the beginning of his academic career, studying diplomatic history under Harold Temperley in the 1920s – the relationship between government and history; more specifically, the efforts he believed that every government in every era made to bend history to its own purposes. It was a preoccupation expressed most succinctly in a letter to A.J.P. Taylor in August 1949, in which

[10] Richard J. Aldrich, 'Policing the past: Official history, secrecy and British intelligence since 1945', *English Historical Review*, cxix (Sept. 2004), 922–53. In this article Professor Aldrich writes (p. 929): 'The person who came closest to sounding the alarm was Sir Herbert Butterfield. Ten years after the war [*sic*] he issued a strident warning about such official history. Well-connected, but ultimately denied an opportunity to join the privileged ranks of official historians, Butterfield in all probability knew about the *Ultra* secret. He warned: "I must say that I do not personally believe there is a government in Europe which wants the public to know the truth." He then explained how the mechanisms of secrecy and government claims of "openness" worked in tandem. "Firstly, that governments press upon the historian the key to all the drawers but one, and are anxious to spread the belief that this single one contains no secret importance: secondly, that if the historian can only find out the thing which the government does not want him to know, he will lay his hand upon something that is likely to be significant." In retrospect, this is a comment on *Ultra* as the "missing dimension" of the official histories the war. It also stands as a salutary warning to scholars working in the wake of any major conflict who feed only upon material available from official sources.' Butterfield was certainly well connected, and it is possible that he was aware of the Ultra secret, but the German diplomatic documents seem a much more immediate and better-documented source for his concern.

[11] This is the title given by Butterfield (*Studies*, p. 129). Michael Kennedy has pointed out (email to author of 6 February 2020) that 'There is no specific "Historical Society" in UCD – the Literary and Historical Society is one of the prestigious debating societies, the History Society is the society for history students and then there is the Ireland-wide Irish Historical Society. To speak at the IHS would be a much bigger deal than at the two former.' On balance, however, I feel that the History Society remains the most probable venue.

[12] McIntire, *Butterfield*, p. 169, states that Butterfield 'arranged with his Irish historian friends to read the piece in Dublin in December 1948, and exacted their promise of immediate publication in an Irish journal'. This is quite possible, although I have discovered no evidence for either of these claims in Butterfield's papers at Cambridge University Library. McIntire enjoyed access to materials, including diaries, that are not publicly available, but the suggestion that Butterfield exacted a promise of immediate publication does not seem to square with his correspondence with the editor of *Studies*: see note 52 below.

he wrote: 'I am as a historian against all governments, or rather I believe that something oblique is going on behind all governments, giving them a seamy side.'[13] Not long before his death thirty years later, in one of the last letters he wrote to his old friend Professor T. Desmond Williams of University College Dublin, Butterfield was still deprecating the efforts of universities 'to please the government of the day' and 'the temptations to give official opportunities, even special facilities for the study of official documents to members of Institutes who will soon tend even to be competing with one another for official favour or special contacts with governments'.[14]

But if this says something about the importance Butterfield attached to official meddling with the historical record, it does not explain the timing of his paper or the nature of its contents; nor the speed with which he turned, in the early months of 1949, to preparing it for publication with a view to circulating it to as many as possible of his academic colleagues. Part of the answer may lie in his hostility to the kind of official history practised by the British government since 1941, when the decision had been taken to record Britain's war effort, both military and – for the first time – civil, in two series of narrative histories edited respectively by Butterfield's Cambridge colleague Professor J.R.M. (later Sir James) Butler and Professor W.K. (later Sir Keith) Hancock.[15] The two series came to occupy the energies of some of the brightest talents of the British historical profession, including Cambridge colleagues close to Butterfield: Michael Postan (a Fellow of Peterhouse) and Betty Behrens (a Fellow of Newnham College), whose decision to join the Cabinet Office's programme provoked Butterfield's bitter opposition because of the harm it would do to her professional career (in which he was proved right); because she would be reneging on her teaching commitments in Cambridge; but also, crucially, because she would be writing 'from sources over whose provision she would

[13] Butterfield to Taylor, 2 August 1949, Cambridge University Library, Butterfield papers, BUTT/130/4 (material from this collection is hereafter cited as BUTT). The 'seamy side' recurs in Butterfield's letter to W.N. Medlicott of 8 August 1949, BUTT/130/4.

[14] Butterfield to Williams, 3 May 1978 (unsigned draft), BUTT/531/W/385. It is impossible to tell whether this draft was actually sent.

[15] For the origins of the War Cabinet's official histories programme, see S.S. Wilson, *The Cabinet Office to 1945* (Public Records Handbook No. 17, London, 1975), pp. 122–30 ('The Historical Section'). For the military series specifically, see Noble Frankland, *History at War* (London, 1998), pp. 40–3; for the civil series, Jose Harris, 'Thucydides amongst the mandarins: Hancock and the World War II civil histories', in *Keith Hancock: The Legacies of an Historian*, ed. D.A. Low (Carlton, Victoria, 2001), pp. 122–48.

have no control'.[16] Michael Bentley is probably right when he writes that 'His violent postwar attack on the entire concept of official history has a personal edge one rarely finds in Butterfield's published work and Betty surely provided the stimulus for it.'[17]

Yet none of the wartime civil histories had appeared by the time Butterfield published his *Studies* article (although the first, *British War Economy*, by Keith Hancock and Margaret Gowing, actually came out in June 1949); and the article paid no attention to narrative history at all (unless one counts a single reference to an unnamed publication by the Ministry of Information). It was the publication by governments of diplomatic documents that preoccupied Butterfield and made his Dublin talk and *Studies* article a matter of such urgency. And here two contexts are important: one general, the other much more specific.

Publishing the diplomatic record of the inter-war period

The general context is the revival of the practice of editing diplomatic documents at the end of the Second World War. The 1920s had seen a great proliferation of publishing projects purporting to illuminate the diplomatic background to the catastrophe of 1914 and, more immediately, to justify the conduct of the various governments involved. It began with the Bolshevik publication of documents from the tsarist era and reached its apogee with the monumental *Die Grosse Politik der europäischen Kabinette 1871–1914*, published in fifty-four volumes between 1922 and 1927, which quickly became notorious for its tendentious presentation of German policy. The British response, *British Documents on the Origins of the War 1898–1914*, was edited by Butterfield's two most important academic mentors: his doctoral supervisor, the domineering and irascible Harold Temperley, and the kindly G.P. Gooch who, as external examiner, had been instrumental in the decision to award Butterfield a first-class degree. The series appeared in eleven volumes between 1924 and 1938, coinciding, therefore, with the first decade and a half of Butterfield's career as a Cambridge don.

At the end of a second conflict two new documentary series were launched. Both derived largely from the initiative of E.L. Woodward, Fellow of All Souls College, Oxford, who had been seconded to the Foreign Office since 1939 but had been closely associated with the Office on previous

[16] Bentley, *Butterfield*, p. 161. Postan's *British War Production* appeared in 1952; Behrens's *Merchant Shipping and the Demands of War* in 1955. With some exceptions, all official histories were published by Her Majesty's Stationery Office, London, until the privatization of HMSO in 1996.

[17] Bentley, *Butterfield*, p. 161.

tasks.[18] *Documents on British Foreign Policy 1919–1939* (DBFP), announced by the Foreign Secretary, Anthony Eden, in March 1944, was the outcome of a prolonged campaign by Woodward to counter the influence first of German and later of American documentary publications, and to ensure that, as Eden put it, the British case should not 'go by default'.[19] Edited by Woodward and his All Souls colleague Rohan Butler, volumes in the first two series, covering the period 1919–38, started to appear in 1946–8, while a new third series, covering the period between the Anschluss and the outbreak of war, was initiated in 1949. Controversy accompanied the project in its early years, beginning with A.J.P. Taylor's notorious (and nominally anonymous) review of the first volume of the second series in the *TLS* of 12 April 1947 which drew a derogatory comparison between the editorial independence of Woodward and Butler and that of Gooch and Temperley.[20] Taylor also criticized their decision to print only official despatches and telegrams, with no letters and no internal Foreign Office minutes – points, incidentally, that were not original but had been suggested to him by the editor of the *TLS*, Stanley Morison. In the furore that followed, Morison lost his job and Taylor was obliged to withdraw the accusation of lack of independence; but Woodward ('a skilled intriguer', according to Taylor) never forgave him.[21] The affair touched on Butterfield's deepest academic and filial loyalties as well as reinforcing his suspicion that 'our "official historians" were becoming accomplices in an effort to lull us to sleep'.[22] For Butterfield, perpetual vigilance was imperative.

The discovery of a huge cache of documents from the German Foreign Office by Allied troops in March–April 1945 led to a second Woodward initiative when, in November 1945, Butterfield proposed the publication of an authoritative record of German foreign policy based on these and other relevant German

---

[18] Uri Bialer, 'Telling the truth to the people: Britain's decision to publish the diplomatic papers of the inter-war period', *Historical Journal*, xxvi (June 1983), 349–67; Peter J. Beck, 'Locked in a dusty cupboard, neither accessible on the policy-makers' desks nor cleared for early publication: Llewellyn Woodward's official diplomatic history of the Second World War', *English Historical Review*, cxxvii (Dec. 2012), 1435–70.

[19] Cabinet paper of 24 January 1944, quoted in ibid., p. 1438.

[20] 'The secrets of diplomacy', in *Struggles for Supremacy*, ed. Wrigley, pp. 161–7.

[21] For accounts of the affair, see A.J.P. Taylor, *A Personal History* (London, 1984), p. 232; Kathleen Burk, *Troublemaker: The Life and History of A.J.P. Taylor* (New Haven and London, 2000), pp. 271–2, and p. 453, note 111; Foreign and Commonwealth Office (FCO) Historians, *History at the Heart of Diplomacy: Historians in the Foreign Office, 1918–2018* (History Note No. 22, London, 2018), p. 26 <https://issuu.com/fcohistorians/docs/history_at_the_heart_of_diplomacy-w>.

[22] *Studies*, p. 137; *Human Relations*, p. 206.

archives.[23] The proposal derived from Woodward's fear, shared with Namier, that the Germans might seek to influence interpretations of the origins of this second war, just as they had done with the *Grosse Politik* in the 1920s.[24] At first conceived as a four-power project, it became an Anglo-American one when the Soviets refused to participate, with an agreement signed on 19 June 1946; the French government subsequently joined the project in April 1947. The German Foreign Office archives were held first at Marburg and later in Berlin; but in the autumn of 1948, during the Soviet blockade of the western zones of the city, they were evacuated, along with the multinational editorial team, to Whaddon Hall in Buckinghamshire, part of the wartime Bletchley Park complex.[25] Each country appointed an editor-in-chief, a position held first for the United Kingdom by John Wheeler-Bennett, then jointly by James Joll and General Sir James Marshall-Cornwall from June to December 1948, then by Sir James alone until 1951.[26]

The first volumes in the series *Documents on German Foreign Policy 1918–1945* (DGFP) started to appear in English from 1949 and in German from 1950 onwards. If the test for the British series was whether it met the high standards set by Gooch and Temperley, the German series evoked a different kind of disquiet on Butterfield's part. He had deep respect for German historical scholarship and had many friends among the German academic community, some encountered during a controversial lecture tour of German universities in 1938.[27] If German scholars could not be trusted to publish their diplomatic documents with sufficient detachment, would American, British or French scholars – scholars who were, in Butterfield's words, engaged in 'the most subtle of all historical tasks, the selection of such of the diplomatic documents of the defeated power as we shall allow to be published to the world'[28] – do a better job? When he wrote those words

---

[23] Paul R. Sweet, 'Der Versuch amtlicher Einflussnahme auf die Edition der "Documents on German Foreign Policy, 1933–1941". Ein Fall aus den fünfziger Jahren', *Vierteljahrshefte für Zeitgeschichte*, xxxix (Apr. 1991), 265–303; Sacha Zala, *Geschichte unter der Schere politischer Zensur. Amtliche Aktensammlungen im internationalen Vergleich* (Munich, 2001); Astrid M. Eckert, *The Struggle for the Files: The Western Allies and the Return of German Archives after the Second World War* (New York, 2012).

[24] Eckert, *Struggle for the Files*, p. 35.

[25] Sweet, 'Einflussnahme', pp. 270–1; Zala, *Geschichte*, pp. 163–6; George O. Kent, 'The German Foreign Ministry's archives at Whaddon Hall, 1948–58', *American Archivist*, xxiv (1961), 43–54.

[26] Sir John Wheeler-Bennett, *Friends, Enemies and Sovereigns* (London, 1976), pp. 58–92. Details of editors, with their dates of service, are given at the beginning of each volume of DGFP.

[27] Bentley, *Butterfield*, pp. 119–46.

[28] *Studies*, p. 133; *Human Relations*, p. 192. For German reactions to the Allied project see Eckert, *Struggle for the Files*, pp. 295–302.

Butterfield knew what he was talking about, for he had a direct line to the heart of the German document project.

Desmond Williams and the German documents

That direct line, and the second, more immediate context for Butterfield's worries about official history, was provided by one man: Desmond Williams. Butterfield had succeeded Temperley as external examiner to the Irish universities in 1938 and the attractions of wartime visits to congenial colleagues in neutral Ireland more than made up for the arduous duties the job entailed.[29] He had first encountered Williams as an outstandingly able student at University College Dublin (UCD). In 1944, impressed by his 'amazing' master's thesis on the rise of National Socialism and by a precocious devotion to German scholarship as fervent as his own,[30] Butterfield persuaded Williams to read for a PhD in Cambridge.[31] Despite, or perhaps because of, Williams's chaotic personal habits and unorthodox political views, a close friendship soon developed.[32] Things went wrong, however, in 1947 when Butterfield tried to get Williams elected as a Bye-Fellow at Peterhouse. The Master of the College, Paul Vellacott, vetoed the appointment, probably because of a notorious incident in which a drunken Williams and an equally drunken undergraduate, Colin Welch, had played a practical joke on an unpopular bursar. Welch was sent down; Williams

---

[29] Bentley, *Butterfield*, pp. 136–7, 166–7.

[30] Butterfield to Williams, 1 March 1945, BUTT/231/W/203.

[31] His subject was 'Pan-Germanism in Austria, 1898–1902', under the supervision of Charles Crawley at Trinity Hall: McGuire, 'Williams', p. 4; Bentley, *Butterfield*, p. 240.

[32] Bentley, *Butterfield*, p. 163. See also pp. 166–7, 240–1, 277. Desmond Williams gave rise to endless stories, many to do with his alleged sympathies for Nazi Germany. According to Michael Bentley, he 'frequently carried in his jacket (they say) a signed photograph of the Führer' (p. 163). The story I heard was that the teenage Williams conducted a correspondence with Josef Goebbels from his Dublin sickbed (he suffered throughout his life from the consequences of a childhood accident). Dermot Keogh's suggestion – in *Ireland and Europe 1919–1948* (Dublin and Totowa, NJ, 1988), p. 243 – that he was a 'member of British intelligence during the Second World War' seems to be a misapprehension based on a photograph of Williams in British uniform, presumably dating from his time as an editor of the German diplomatic documents in Berlin in 1947–8 (I am grateful to Dr Michael Kennedy for this information). It is confirmed by an obituary which states that, as an editor in Berlin, Williams bore 'a nominal military rank': James McGuire, 'T. Desmond Williams (1921–87)', *Irish Historical Studies*, xxvi (May 1988), 3–7 (p. 4).

escaped unscathed, but paid the price with the end of his Peterhouse career.[33]

In September 1947, on the rebound from Peterhouse and on Butterfield's recommendation (probably to James Passant, the Foreign Office librarian whom he knew well as a former medievalist at Sidney Sussex College, Cambridge), Williams took a job with the British Foreign Office team editing the German documents in Berlin. He remained there until the autumn of 1948 when, along with the rest of the editorial team, he was evacuated to Whaddon Hall. Here he was only a short train journey from Cambridge and he visited Butterfield often over the winter of 1948–9. He also spoke to him frequently on the telephone and wrote a number of letters. These letters, written first from Berlin and Dublin, and later from Whaddon Hall, represent only a small element of an intensely close personal and intellectual relationship, but provide important clues to what they were talking about.[34] Williams's first and only letter from Berlin was undated but probably written some time during the period of growing tension before the imposition of the Soviet blockade on 18 June 1948 because, he said, there was 'serious doubt whether we can remain in Berlin much longer'.[35] Much of this long letter was devoted to ruminations on the Peterhouse debacle of the previous year, but there was also much positive news about the editorial project, not least because it promised to overturn orthodox views on the origins of the war:

> The work is quite fascinating from our viewpoint. We here in Berlin owing to the failure of Wheeler-B to keep in contact have been given complete responsibility in the final selection of Vol 1 & 2. This goes to some extent to satisfy my personal doubts on the 'ethics' of this present post, and I feel that when these volumes appear at the end of the year, they will not be open to the accusation of partisan selection. In brief the results tend to rehabilitate Neville C and Halifax and most of the permanent staff of the F.O. (always

---

[33] Colin Welch later became a successful journalist with the *Daily Telegraph*, launching its 'Way of the World' column and serving as deputy editor for sixteen years. A footnote to Welch's obituary in the *Peterhouse Annual Record 2011/2012* (Peterhouse, Cambridge, 2016), p. 119 (note 12) gives a different, less dramatic version of the incident. James McGuire's obituary gives an inaccurate account of the circumstances of Williams's departure from Cambridge: McGuire, 'Williams', p. 4.

[34] The letters were divided by Butterfield into two separate files: his 'official history' file, now BUTT/130 in the Butterfield papers, and his much larger file of personal correspondence, now BUTT/531. The sequence can be understood only by juxtaposing the two. McIntire, *Butterfield*, pp. 169–70, has done this and he provides a useful brief account of the episode, though erring when he states that it was the *start* of Butterfield's friendship with Williams.

[35] Williams to Butterfield, n.d. (1948), BUTT/531/W/202A.

excluding Vansittart).[36] A quandary which has caused great pain to our American colleagues is the fact that the documents of the 'professional' German diplomats display considerable integrity, very sound judgement, and immense courage in their reports and despatches back to the Wilhelmstrasse. Even such an organisation as the Auslandsorganisation of the Party (which possessed a separate department of the F.O. since 1937) is shown to be quite innocent of most of the charges levelled against it. Of 5th columnist stories, etc. there is almost a complete absence.

Williams also had time for his own research. His 'hopes as to the possibility of utilising the pre-1914 documents' had been fulfilled; the libraries were 'wonderful'; and he had had several meetings with leading historians, including Friedrich Meinecke ('a grand old failing giant'), Gerhard Ritter and Ulrich Noack.[37] But he already had severe reservations about the German document project, and they centred on two figures whose names were to recur through his subsequent correspondence. One was the American editor-in-chief, Raymond J. Sontag; the other was E.L. Woodward. With Sontag the issue focused on the American decision to publish, without prior warning to their allies, a separate volume of documents, *Nazi–Soviet Relations 1939–1941*. Appearing in January 1948 as a propaganda instrument in the intensifying Cold War, the volume provoked anger on the part of their British and French colleagues, and indeed of the British Foreign Secretary, Ernest Bevin.[38] Williams gave a concise account of the affair:

> I had hoped to return to England sooner – but the necessities occasioned by premature American publication of War Documents and the consequential

[36] Sir Robert Vansittart, permanent under-secretary for foreign affairs, 1930–8; chief diplomatic adviser, 1938–40. Williams was later to make exactly the same criticism of DBFP: see p. 48 below.

[37] All three historians were conservative and nationalist, and all had had complicated relationships with the Nazi regime. Both Ritter and Noack had been briefly imprisoned following the July 1944 bomb plot. However, Noack (1899–1974) had been closest to the regime, having joined the Party in 1939, and having facilitated a visit by the Norwegian National Socialist leader Vidkun Quisling to Berlin in December of that year: see Hans Fredrik Dahl, *Quisling: A Study in Treachery* (Cambridge, 1999), pp. 145–50. In the 1950s Noack became a prominent advocate of a united, neutralized Germany; he ended as a supporter of the German Social Democratic Party (SPD): see <https://ns-zeit.uni-greifswald.de/projekt/personen/noack-ulrich> for a concise survey of his career. Noack and Butterfield had shared interests in Machiavelli and Lord Acton (on whom Noack had written his *Habilitationsschrift* in 1936); after the war they visited each other in Cambridge and Würzburg. Butterfield's post-war correspondence with Noack is in BUTT 52–4, and with Ritter in BUTT 57.

[38] Wheeler-Bennett, *Friends*, pp. 84–6; Zala, *Geschichte*, pp. 210–26; Eckert, *Struggle for the Files*, pp. 92–4.

'propaganda' have kept me in Berlin … Sontag has certainly produced a remarkable volume which even in the eyes of the F.O. is a peculiarly disgraceful exhibition of 'la trahison des clercs'. I do not know whether you have read the State Department book on Russo-German relations, but it contains no fewer than 501 translation errors!!! … As usual, Sontag produced his work without consulting his colleagues and Bevin's somewhat sharp criticism is if anything too light. Wheeler B and Renouvin are, I must say, taking a sound historical line.[39]

It is not easy to see exactly what Woodward had done to annoy Williams, but the latter's hostility is clear:

Sontag horrified his colleagues by complaining that the material relating to [?Austria] is all too favourable to Hitler, and that we had better drop it altogether. He also expressed a worry that Congress should blame him for financing a production which if anything might overthrow the historical version of 1939 which inspired many of its actions.[40] According to Wheeler Bennett, Woodward – although not directly involved, has also in the matter of advice, taken a most peculiar line, and indeed I am not surprised after reading his Inaugural Lecture of 1945.[41] However, as you once wisely remarked – these propagandists will let the cat out of the bag with their various feuds, and thereby leave for future historians the denied material. In one sense, it is much better that they should all quarrel, and seem to blacken each other.

Apart from a single letter from Dublin, written in May 1948 ('I shall not forget to post you the reference on Woodward'),[42] all of Williams's six remaining letters were sent from Whaddon Hall. The timing of these letters is important. They fall into three phases: two in November and early December 1948, in other words the time when Butterfield was

[39] The distinguished diplomatic historian Pierre Renouvin was the first French editor-in-chief. He resigned from the project early in 1948 and was succeeded by Maurice Baumont: Eckert, *Struggle for the Files*, p. 91; Zala, *Geschichte*, p. 232.

[40] Yet Sontag was equally suspicious of the intentions of his British colleagues, fearing that they were attempting to suppress files that cast an unfavourable light on Britain's policy of appeasement: Eckert, *Struggle for the Files*, p. 92.

[41] E.L. Woodward, *The Study of International Relations at a University: An Inaugural Lecture Delivered before the University of Oxford on 17 February 1945* (Oxford, 1945). Williams may have been referring here to Woodward's criticism of the claim of *Die Grosse Politik* to offer an objective record of German foreign policy before 1914 (ibid., pp. 14–15); or to his condemnation of the German historical profession for its willingness to toe the National Socialist line: 'how is it that the *Historische Zeitschrift*, with its tradition of exact scholarship, should have found German historians of former repute willing to contribute to it after it had begun to print fatuous as well as poisonous rubbish about the Jewish question?' (ibid., p. 18).

[42] Williams to Butterfield, 14 May 1948, BUTT/531/W/204.

preparing his talk for University College Dublin; two in March 1949, after Butterfield's article had been sent to press but before it had been published – these contained Williams's most alarming allegations about the German document project – and a final pair in July 1949, when Williams was on the verge of leaving the German editorial team.

We can picture Butterfield trying to put together the paper he had promised UCD. As usual, he would have been overworked and overcommitted, turning his mind to official history after completing his gruelling series of lectures on Christianity and history to the Cambridge Divinity School, probably by the end of November; and having barely a fortnight before he sailed to Dublin on 8 December, to deliver his paper on the 14th. Williams wrote to him on 23 November:

> I send you by parcel post today 'Nazi–Soviet Relations – 1939–41' published by the State Dept. The editors are working with us on the Documents but we take no responsibility for this 'separate' production.
>
> I do not think it would be wise to be concrete in any remarks on the forthcoming volumes or on the Woodward plot over the Halifax letter until it is actually hatched. The defects of Sontag's production can easily be gleaned from a hasty perusal. Note particularly the choice of time for the first documents, and the omission of the previous history of Soviet–British relations. The references in the German documents to them are also omitted. I send you the Russian comment (in German).
>
> I hope in the next day or two (but it may be difficult) to send you the original Russian Document[s] themselves which they have published from the German papers.[43]

Again, what Williams thought about *Nazi–Soviet Relations* is clear; it is not so easy to discover what he meant about 'the Woodward plot over the Halifax letter'.[44] Expressing his thanks on 3 December, Butterfield was uncertain whether the two volumes were confidential (rather surprisingly in the American case, since *Nazi–Soviet Relations* was to become one of the State Department's greatest publishing successes)[45] and asked whether, if he commented on them, 'would this be irregular, and should I be in danger of giving you away[?]'.[46] On the eve of Butterfield's departure for Ireland, Williams replied: 'Thank you for the quick return of the books. I shall

[43] Williams to Butterfield, 23 November 1948, BUTT/531/W/205.

[44] On this point, Williams may have been in agreement with Sontag (note 38 above) in suspecting British efforts to suppress evidence of British appeasement of Hitler.

[45] Zala, *Geschichte*, p. 226.

[46] Butterfield to Williams, 3 December 1948, BUTT/531/W/206.

bring you in person the Russian volumes which have now been translated into English. They are not "confidential".'[47] He added that he would be travelling to Ireland on 11–12 December and returning on the 13th, 'if I get my 24 hours leave': in other words, he would not be present when Butterfield gave his paper at UCD.

Williams's contributions duly found their way into Butterfield's paper, along with a miscellany of other examples including wartime publications from the Ministry of Information, military despatches and, most importantly, the editorial practices of Gooch and Temperley. There were two extended references to *Nazi–Soviet Relations*. One questioned the independence of the editors – about which, he said, the book's preface and editors' foreword seemed to 'protest too much'.[48] The second reference, on the other hand, praised the editors for including the statement that 'Each document has been printed in full, without omissions or alterations.'[49] This, he felt, was firmer than 'a mere guarantee that nothing "relevant" or "important" had been omitted' (presumably a dig at the editors of DBFP).[50] Butterfield's other reference to the German document project followed one of several unfavourable comparisons between DBFP and its predecessors, focusing once again on the editors' decision not to publish internal Foreign Office minutes: 'We shall be alert to discover whether the same principles are adopted in the publication of the captured German documents.'[51]

Publishing 'Pitfalls'

Early in 1949 Father P.J. Connolly SJ, the editor of *Studies*, wrote to Butterfield inviting him to publish his paper on 'contemporary history' in his journal.[52] At first sight, a quarterly review published by the Irish Province of the Society of Jesus was not the best vehicle to reach a large audience in the United Kingdom, despite its important place in the intellectual life of the Republic. But it offered the possibility of early publication – as early as the March 1949 issue – and, when he wrote on 16 February to accept Connolly's offer, Butterfield requested fifty offprints in order to 'get into

[47] Williams to Butterfield, 7 December 1948, BUTT/531/W/207.

[48] *Studies*, p. 133; *Human Relations*, p. 192.

[49] Both the preface and the editors' foreword can be found in the complete edition of *Nazi–Soviet Relations* published on the Avalon Project website: <https://avalon.law.yale.edu/subject_menus/nazsov.asp>.

[50] *Studies*, p. 134. When revising the paper for *History and Human Relations*, however, he added a new final sentence to the paragraph: 'The time has also come when assurances of this kind must be absolutely specific.' *Human Relations*, p. 199.

[51] *Studies*, p. 138.

[52] Since there is no letter from Connolly in BUTT/130, this is deduced from Butterfield's acceptance letter (note 53 below).

the hands of historians, many of whom will not be readers of *Studies*'.[53] Butterfield moved quickly, sending his manuscript on 20 February; but not quickly enough to make the March issue.[54] However, delay until June gave him an opportunity to make two late additions.[55] One was actually included as a footnote to his manuscript in order, he said, 'to do justice to a new volume [of DBFP] which seems to have followed the rules better';[56] the other, requested on 7 March when the article was already at proof stage, had to be appended as a lengthy 'PS'.[57] Both additions offer insights into the thoughts troubling Butterfield's mind in the interval between the delivery of his paper in December 1948 and early March 1949.

The footnote (published on page 135 of the article) called a temporary truce with Woodward and Butler. As we have seen, Butterfield shared (albeit less stridently) Taylor's doubts about their editorial independence and their decision not to publish Foreign Office minutes. In his footnote Butterfield took the opportunity to acknowledge a change in practice in subsequent volumes of DBFP which, his view, marked a welcome return to the policy of Gooch and Temperley regarding the inclusion of Foreign Office minutes and an explicit declaration of editorial independence.

The second addition, also intended as a footnote if it had not arrived too late, again seemed to hark back to the era of Gooch and Temperley, since it would have been added to the section (page 131 in the published version) where Butterfield discussed Temperley's views on 'the decline of frankness' in British diplomacy between the time of Canning and Palmerston and that of Sir Edward Grey. Butterfield's postscript indeed began with Temperley. But the perspective shifted quickly to a different subject. The German document project had now become the focus of his deepest suspicions of governmental interference. Butterfield demanded the utmost vigilance on the part of the editors in pursuit of any gaps they might suspect in the documentation, insisting that they should not say they had seen documents when they had only seen photostats, 'possibly reduced in number after re-photographing in some allied government department':[58]

It is essential that the editors, if they suspect the existence of further documents,

---

[53] Butterfield to Connolly, 16 February, BUTT/130/4.

[54] Butterfield to Connolly, 20 February, BUTT/130/4.

[55] Both were later adapted and incorporated into the version published in *History and Human Relations*.

[56] Ibid.

[57] Butterfield to Connolly, 7 March 1949, BUTT/130/4.

[58] Given the vagaries of Allied (and wartime German) microfilming efforts, this was a valid fear. See Eckert, *Struggle for the Files*, pp. 62–4.

should pursue them remorselessly and, if they fail to find them, should give an account of this, guarding the historical student rather than officialdom.

Butterfield concluded by resuming his altercation with the editors of DBFP, acknowledging their vigilance in pursuing missing telegrams but returning to the charge that the decision not to publish minutes and memoranda meant that 'the enquiry is cut off (so far as the public is concerned) at the critical points'. And his final sentence hinted cryptically at mysteries still to be revealed:

> We shall also learn from our own publications of the German documents how far the real secrets of foreign offices are to be found in the formal diplomatic correspondence and how far it is true that the really revealing documents are the ones which, in the case of the British Foreign Office, are being withheld.

Williams sounds the alarm

What prompted this late addition, with its intimation that documents were being deliberately held back from publication in both the German and the British series, and its insistence that the editors should see the original documents and not photostats? What, in other words, had Desmond Williams been saying? It would be tempting at this point to engage in the kind of historical 'reconstruction' that Butterfield compared (in a paragraph omitted from the revised version)[59] to a detective story – a genre to which he was addicted. In this case, however, we cannot play Sherlock Holmes confounding Scotland Yard because what looks at first sight like the key piece of evidence, 'so pivotal in character that it governs the interpretation of the other clues, and then produces a new map of the whole affair', turned up a full two weeks after Butterfield had submitted his final revision to the editor. It arrived in the form of a letter from Williams dated 24 March 1949: the first he had written to Butterfield since early December. The letter is worth quoting in full:

> My dear Herbert,
>
> A hurried line. I and [sic] 2 of my colleagues are considering resigning if suspicions we have very recently entertained prove to be correct. This is at present in the realm of hypothesis – but we are pretty certain that the F.O. has contrary to solemn (if evasive) assurance has [sic] withheld 400 documents on Anglo-German relations which they have stated were missing from the original German collection when found.

---

[59] *Studies*, p. 137.

I would like to discuss the whole matter thoroughly with you and in <u>great</u> confidence. There is no <u>immediate</u> rush but I could come to Cambridge the week-end following this coming one – in early April.

It is indeed an appalling story – if true – and indication of the <u>incompetent</u> villainy of official historians.

With good wishes as ever

Yours

Desmond

P.S. Please excuse this brevity – but it is a long story and the post calls.

The date of the letter means that it cannot be the source of the anxieties expressed in Butterfield's additions to his article. It must nonetheless have reinforced suspicions already in his mind and probably fostered by further exchanges with Williams between Christmas 1948 and early March 1949 of which we have no written record: suspicions that undoubtedly prompted the postscript to his article.[60] Indeed, this is confirmed by a conciliatory letter to Woodward, written after the *Studies* article had appeared, when Butterfield told him that 'my question about the mechanics of selecting the documents happened to be concerned (in my thoughts)[61] not so much with your series as with the German series, which presents a case where the Foreign Office might[62] not trust all the people assisting it as much as it would trust you'.[63]

Williams's letter of 24 March 1949 (backed up by a subsequent telephone conversation)[64] must therefore have confirmed Butterfield's suspicions about the German project in the most dramatic way. He took decisive action.

[60] McIntire, *Butterfield*, pp. 169–70, comes to the same conclusion.

[61] The words in parentheses are a handwritten addition.

[62] Handwritten correction of 'would'.

[63] Butterfield to Woodward, 31 July 1949, BUTT/130/4.

[64] As stated in Butterfield's letter to Williams of 1 April (note 65 below). Two undated letters from Williams were probably sent shortly after his letter of 24 March. The first, written on 'Monday' (28 March?) referred to Butterfield's father's illness, which had worsened around this time (Bentley, *Butterfield*, p. 266), confirmed an arrangement to meet in Brewer Street, London, at 1 p.m. on 'Saturday' (2 April?), and concluded: 'I am writing a memo on the subject which I shall post you tomorrow Tuesday. It should reach you Thursday [31 March?]': BUTT/531/W/202. In the second letter Williams wrote: 'I have not sent you the memo – which I have prepared – as I shall be seeing General Marshall-Cornwall tomorrow – and that conversation may render out of date the memo. However I shall have a full written statement for you – when we meet on Saturday. Could you change the time to 1.15 pm?': BUTT/130/4. Whether they met in London on 2 April is unclear, but Butterfield had already responded decisively the previous day.

On 1 April he wrote formally to Williams, copying his letter to the Master of Peterhouse (Vellacott), the Vice-Chancellor of Cambridge University (Charles Raven, a theologian and friend) and James Passant at the Foreign Office.[65] 'If what you describe has been substantiated,' Butterfield wrote, 'in my opinion it is your duty to resign in a signal manner, making the reason as public as possible, and doing this as soon after you have clarified the situation as you can reasonably manage.' For his own part, Butterfield went on, 'I can't think that any possible consequences to myself would deter me from airing a matter so important to the public and to historical science, if the case is such as you describe.'

At very least, Butterfield's injunction to resign on a matter of principle was disingenuous, since he had been plotting for the previous two years to secure Williams a position at University College Dublin: a position that ultimately became nothing less than the new Chair of Modern History. As early as September 1947, the month in which Williams failed to secure the Peterhouse Bye-Fellowship, Butterfield had been discussing with Father Aubrey Gwynn SJ, a lecturer in medieval history at UCD, the possibility that Desmond Williams might be persuaded to return to UCD. At that point, the failure of the college authorities to make a sufficiently attractive offer had led Williams to accept the Foreign Office post.[66] However, the death of the Professor of History, John O'Sullivan,[67] in February 1948 opened an opportunity, Father Gwynn wrote, to adopt 'a new policy of separating the present Chair of History into two independent chairs of Medieval and Modern History'. 'This', he went on, 'is the opportunity for which Des. Williams has, I presume, been waiting; and the probable time-table should suit him well – as new statutes will be required and the two chairs are not likely to be filled before the summer of 1949.'[68] Despite reservations about entrusting 'so big and important a chair to so young a man, without any previous experience of his quality as teacher, examiner or colleague',[69] in June 1948 UCD 'finally decided to act on your advice, take a plunge boldly and appoint him at once to the new Professorship of Modern History'.[70] In the autumn of 1949, at the age of twenty-eight

---

[65] Butterfield to Williams, Vellacott, Raven and Passant, all dated 1 April 1949, BUTT/130/4.

[66] Gwynn to Butterfield, 22 September 1947, BUTT/531/G/80.

[67] '... with his Nazi connections and a less than fulsome view of British policy towards Germany': Bentley, *Butterfield*, p. 167.

[68] Gwynn to Butterfield, 2 March 1948, BUTT/531/G/83.

[69] Ibid.

[70] Gwynn to Butterfield, 18 June 1948, BUTT/531/G/86.

and supported by Butterfield's fulsome reference,[71] Williams took up his appointment, a position he held until 1983. The new Chair of Medieval History was occupied by Father Aubrey Gwynn.

Williams was therefore under no pressure to resign from the editorial team, and there is no sign in Butterfield's papers that he went further to substantiate the allegation that the Foreign Office was deliberately withholding 400, or any number, of documents on Anglo-German relations. Nor did Butterfield put his head above the parapet by 'airing a matter so important to the public and to historical science'.[72] He did, however, have another string to his bow, for his article on the pitfalls of official history in the June 1949 issue of *Studies* was still to appear. And there was definitely substance to Desmond Williams's allegations.

The Windsor papers

In the years between 1945 and 1949, and again between 1953 and 1957, the British government attempted variously to destroy, conceal or prevent the publication of a cluster of documents that told the story of the German government's attempts to influence the Duke and Duchess of Windsor during their journey in 1940 from the south of France through Spain and Portugal to Lisbon, from where the Duke was to sail in order to take up his post as Governor of the Bahamas.[73] The story is familiar and has been extensively discussed, often in sensationalist terms.[74] It represented the British government's only known attempt to interfere with the editorial independence of the German documents project: but that very fact made the challenge a serious one.[75]

The documents in question had been discovered at an early stage in the inspection of 400 tonnes of documents from the German Foreign Office

[71] Of 4 May 1949, BUTT/531/[unnumbered but probably W/207].

[72] He was, however, preoccupied by his father's illness at this time (note 64 above). He was also about to start delivering his lectures on Christianity and history for the BBC (Easter 1949 fell between Thursday 14 and Monday 18 April).

[73] Michael Bloch, *Operation Willi: The Plot to Kidnap the Duke of Windsor, July 1940* (London, 1984).

[74] See the references in Sweet, 'Einflussnahme', p. 266. A fictionalized version of the story featured in the second series of *The Crown* on Netflix.

[75] Paul Sweet's 1991 article marked the beginning of a more scholarly approach to the Duke of Windsor story. It was then pursued by the Swiss historian Sacha Zala, who met Sweet and was given access to his private archive: see Sacha Zala, *Geschichte*, especially pp. 179–83, 194–5, 291–3, 308–9. The most recent account, in Eckert, *Struggle for the Files*, pp. 70–3, draws on Sweet and Zala, but adds important details, some based on British Foreign Office sources. Sweet later published a shorter, English-language version of his article: 'The Windsor file', *The Historian*, lix (1997), 263–79.

discovered at various locations in Thuringia and Lower Saxony in March–April 1945, and moved at the beginning of May to Marburg, north of Frankfurt and well beyond the reach of the advancing Soviet forces. The files were stored in the castle where they were microfilmed, the microfilms then being sent to the Foreign Office in London and the State Department in Washington.[76]

At the Foreign Office, Rohan Butler later recalled, it was Woodward's job to go through the microfilms. 'It happened, though, that Woodward was on leave in July 1945 so that it fell to me to be the first to report on the Windsor documents, as I well remember.'[77] In a collection of documents on Anglo-German relations from the office of Ernst von Weizsäcker, the head of the German Foreign Office, there were several, Butler reported, in which the Duke of Windsor 'appears in a somewhat curious light'.[78] Numerous British attempts to get the relevant items either destroyed or delivered into exclusively British hands were rebuffed by the Americans during the summer and autumn of 1945; but the State Department eventually agreed to keep its microfilm of the Windsor papers under lock and key.[79] This was not the end of the story, however. For in June 1946, as we have seen, the British and American governments accepted Woodward's proposal to publish the German documents. It still required a direct appeal from Wheeler-Bennett to Foreign Secretary Ernest Bevin before they were released,[80] but the Windsor papers eventually took their place among all the other German documents being considered for publication, first in Berlin (to which they were moved from Marburg in January 1946), and later at Whaddon Hall.

But did the Windsor papers form the basis of Desmond Williams's allegation about the withholding of '400 documents on Anglo-German relations'? One man certainly thought so. Paul Sweet, the American diplomatic historian who joined the US editorial team in September 1948 and became its head in 1952, read Butterfield's chapter in *History and Human Relations* with particular interest because he had worked closely with Desmond Williams at Whaddon Hall and knew of the friendship

---

[76] Sweet, 'Einflussnahme', pp. 270–1; Zala, *Geschichte*, pp. 163–6. See Wheeler-Bennett, *Friends*, pp. 82–3, on why the practice of microfilming was abandoned. Some of the files, including the Windsor papers, had already been microfilmed by the Germans: see Eckert, *Struggle for the Files*, pp. 62–4.

[77] Letter from Butler to Heather Yasamee (FCO Library and Records Department), 14 June 1991, FCO Historians' collection.

[78] Minute of 17 July 1945, quoted in Sweet, 'Einflussnahme', p. 271.

[79] Sweet, 'Einflussnahme', p. 273; Zala, *Geschichte*, pp. 179–83.

[80] Wheeler-Bennett, *Friends*, p. 81.

between the two men. He recalled in 1956 that 'when his book came out it seemed to me that, to illustrate the dangers of official history, he might have found better examples than in the tripartite project', adding that 'in this essay Butterfield referred with approval to the procedures of the editors of the German documents, contrasting them, much to the latter's disadvantage, with the practice of Sir Llewellyn Woodward, who, as editor of the British documents, omitted the marginal notes documenting the course of discussion within the Foreign Office'.[81]

When Paul Sweet arrived at Whaddon Hall in September 1948 he already knew about the Windsor documents and assumed that their publication had already been agreed.[82] He was therefore surprised when, some months later, on 15 June 1949, the subject was raised by Malcolm Carroll, the outgoing head of the American team, in a meeting with James Passant, the Foreign Office librarian:

> In the course of a few words of farewell, Carroll, addressing himself to Passant, said: 'The list of documents for 1939–40 is complete, and the editors will soon be able to make the final selection. The documents concerning the Duke of Windsor would then have to be discussed, and he [Carroll] thought that the most important documents should be published.' To this E.J. Passant replied that the documents were available and that, if selected, they would be published. It surprised me that Carroll raised the subject, since I had thought that the question of publication was no longer a matter of dispute. In any case, now, after Passant's reply, the matter must surely be considered closed.[83]

The matter of the Windsor documents must indeed have been closed, presumably to the satisfaction of all present at Whaddon Hall. Evidently, however, some kind of discussion on whether they should be published had been carried on during the preceding months. And it was presumably this that had prompted the alarm raised by Desmond Williams in his letter to Butterfield of 24 March. True, there were nowhere near '400 documents', but the eighteen eventually published still amounted to a substantial collection.[84] Williams may have been referring obliquely to these documents

---

[81] Paul R. Sweet, letter to Professor Raymond J. Sontag, 21 August 1956, quoted in Sweet, 'Einflussnahme', p. 300. Here and in later quotations I use the English translation made by Eleanor Breuning, a British member of the German documents team, for internal Foreign Office use, 29 May 1991 (copy in FCO Historians' collection).

[82] Sweet, 'Einflussnahme', p. 279.

[83] Ibid., p. 279.

[84] *Documents on German Foreign Policy 1918–1945*, series D, vol. X, *The War Years June 23–August 31, 1940* (London, 1957), nos 2, 9, 66, 86, 152, 159, 175, 211, 216, 224, 235, 254, 257, 264, 265, 276, 277, 285.

– he was definitely referring to some kind of improper behaviour on the part of the Foreign Office – when he wrote to Butterfield on 15 July, on the eve of his departure from Whaddon Hall:

> I am indeed most glad to be leaving in a few days this barbaric outfit. I have managed to force the F.O. (at least Passant) to commit himself after much trouble on the questions we have frequently discussed. Did you send him an offprint of your article as there appear to have occurred (on the surface) radical changes in policy[?]. I am quite convinced that Passant is subjectively honest: I also am convinced he has been fooled. The edition we are producing for the Germans is so appalling that I have instructed him not to put my name on the volume concerned – also on our English volume in which the preface is scandalously tendentious, and the footnotes and indices careless beyond belief. I shall bring you advance proof copies for your amusement.[85]

Did 'the questions we have frequently discussed' refer to the Windsor papers? It is quite possible that they did, but it is also possible that he was referring to something much bigger – perhaps much closer to the 400 documents he alleged – for the Windsor papers comprised only the third of three volumes on Anglo-German relations. The first volume, covering the period prior to May 1939 (and therefore including the Munich Agreement) had already disappeared, probably before the end of 1946, and has never been found. Sontag believed that both the first and the third volumes had been deliberately suppressed by the British[86] – and, as we have seen, the third (Windsor) volume was restored in 1947 only at the insistence of the British editor-in-chief.

Butterfield never referred to the missing documents in either the two versions of his official history article or anywhere else, and he seems to have been anxious to cover both Williams's tracks and his own. Williams's letter of 15 July would have arrived at the same time as Butterfield was taking delivery of the offprints of his *Studies* article. He had not sent a copy to Passant, but he appears to have done so immediately after receiving Williams's letter. For in Butterfield's 'official history' file there is a draft covering letter to Passant dated 16 July 1949: it is not clear whether a final version was sent. Handwritten and with a large section crossed out, it is

---

[85] Williams to Butterfield, 15 July 1949, BUTT/531/W207A. Williams's criticisms of DGFP's editorial standards are echoed in Gerhard L. Weinberg, 'Critical note on the *Documents on German Foreign Policy, 1918–1945*', *Journal of Modern History*, xxiii (1951), 38–40.

[86] Sontag, letter of 2 January 1947, quoted in Eckert, *Struggle for the Files*, p. 92. Interestingly, a letter from a US official noting the disappearance of this volume is dated 22 March 1948, only two days before Williams's letter to Butterfield.

more than usually apologetic in tone and reluctant to cause offence. It reads in part:

> It must seem pompous and over-important if I send a covering letter with the enclosed; but owing to your Foreign Office position I had misgivings about sending it, lest it should look like a naughty, provocative, arrogant school-boy-gesture; while I was equally concerned that if you should happen to hear of it from anybody else, my not sending it would seem careless and not very friendly. I can't pretend that you ought to be burdened with it but I think I ought to send it to you – which I do privately, not in your official capacity.[87]

Whether the letter was sent or not, it confirms Butterfield's ambivalent state of mind at the time his article was published.[88] Having poked a stick into the hornet's nest of official history, he was fearful of getting stung by the reaction of 'people whom I like and have reason to be grateful to' (as he put it in the deleted section of his draft). Williams seems to have been equally apprehensive that he had gone too far. Congratulating Butterfield on his article ('I have not read better on the subject ever'), he 'regret[ted] deeply that a comparatively unknown journal like *Studies* should have captured it. However perhaps for me it was better!'[89] Nevertheless, the story of the Windsor documents seemed to have reached a satisfactory conclusion with the decision that they would be published. Butterfield and Williams were not to know that within a few years the threat to suppress them would be repeated at an even higher level.

There is no space to recount the full story here, except to note that it began in July 1953 and involved both the British Prime Minister, Winston Churchill, and the US President, Dwight D. Eisenhower; but that the real impetus to prevent publication of the Windsor documents came from the recently widowed Queen Elizabeth the Queen Mother, abetted by Wheeler-Bennett, now the official biographer of the late King George VI, who had evidently been persuaded to change sides.[90] While the American editorial team resisted strongly, in Britain the brunt was borne by the Hon. Margaret Lambert, who had taken over as editor-in-chief in 1951. The matter was not finally resolved until 1957, when volume X of series D of DGFP was published.[91] It included all eighteen Windsor documents: by this time too many people in the United States, Germany and elsewhere

---

[87] Butterfield to Passant, 16 July 1949 (draft), BUTT/130/4.

[88] Passant did receive the article. In his letter of thanks of 8 August he suggested meeting in Cambridge to discuss it: BUTT/130/4.

[89] Williams to Butterfield, 15 July 1949, BUTT/531/W207A.

[90] Sweet, 'Einflussnahme', pp. 295–6.

[91] Note 84 above.

knew of their existence for concealment to be possible any longer, and the British government had to be satisfied with a disclaimer downplaying the importance of the documents and emphasizing that the Duke of Windsor 'never wavered in his loyalty to the British cause'.[92] Margaret Lambert's private papers provide a unique insight into the affair, including the only known copy of her report of her meeting with Churchill on 16 September 1953.[93] More importantly for our purpose, however, they provide conclusive evidence that Desmond Williams knew what was going on. On 9 July 1953 Lambert wrote to the Permanent Under-Secretary at the Foreign Office, Sir William Strang, reporting a conversation with Professor Bernadotte Schmitt, US editor-in-chief from July 1949 to July 1952. 'Speaking, he said, as a sincere friend of this country', Schmitt 'most strongly advise[d] against any attempt to withhold or even delay, publication of these papers' and adduced many arguments in support of that advice, including the following:

> He also reminded me that a former member of the editorial staff was now in Dublin. He had suspected him before of making trouble for his old colleagues and was convinced he would do it again if we gave him any sort of handle.[94]

This warning did not prevent Schmitt from having lunch with Desmond Williams when he met him in Dublin a few days later.[95] Between 1949 and 1953, however, the Windsor affair had lain dormant, offering Williams no opportunity to make trouble. And it was precisely in that interval that Butterfield had revised his official history article for publication in *History and Human Relations*. The alarmist notes about the German document project sounded in the original article were absent from the revised version. It will be recalled that in 1949, when discussing the absence of minutes in the published British documents, he had written: 'We shall be alert to discover whether the same principles are adopted in the publication of the captured German documents.'[96] By 1951 this had become:

> Some of us waited jealously to see whether in the case of the publication of the captured German documents the same principles would be adopted as have been employed in the selection of our own diplomatic papers. They have not;

---

[92] Sweet, 'Einflussnahme', p. 296.

[93] Lambert to the Marquess of Salisbury (acting foreign secretary), 17 September 1953, Lambert papers (private collection).

[94] Lambert to Strang, 9 July 1953, Lambert papers (private collection). Strang replied the same day, noting that he had 'taken the liberty of sending a copy of it [i.e. her letter] to Chartwell': ibid.

[95] Schmitt to Lambert, 16 July 1953 (from Cork, waiting to sail from Cobh on the *Mauretania*): ibid.

[96] *Studies*, p. 138.

and those who care to disentangle the ordinary diplomatic correspondence from the more confidential type of document in the volumes of German papers can judge the measure of the importance of the revelations which only come from the particular kind of material that we are here discussing.[97]

This was why Paul Sweet was surprised by Butterfield's choice of DGFP to illustrate the dangers of official history. From Butterfield's point of view, *Documents on German Foreign Policy* was a model of official history at its best. Published in 1951, his chapter in *History and Human Relations* ironically gave a more reassuring picture of the German documents project than the facts warranted.

[97] *Human Relations*, p. 204.

2. Butterfield and official history

Butterfield and the historians

By mid-July 1949 Butterfield was busy distributing offprints of his *Studies* article to many of the most eminent members of the British historical profession (Lewis Namier seems to have been a notable omission), and he was soon receiving their replies. Most of them were standard, expressing gratitude, interest and so on.[1] Patrick Bury wrote from Corpus Christi College, Cambridge: 'It reinforces me in my hope that I shall never myself become an "official" or "independent" historian!' Some years later he was to become one of the editors of *Documents on British Foreign Policy.* Among those who sent more substantial replies were E.L. Woodward, W.N. Medlicott, the official historian of the Ministry of Economic Warfare during the Second World War (a fact of which Butterfield, strangely, was unaware when he sent him his offprint) and A.J.P. Taylor.

It is not surprising that Taylor was the one most in sympathy with Butterfield's views, thanking him for having highlighted the 'dangers' of official history and recalling the furore that had surrounded his critical review of the first volume of the second series of DBFP in 1947.[2] He did, however, 'disagree strongly' with Butterfield's idealized view of the international historians of the 1920s, whose impartiality Butterfield had contrasted with the ideologically coloured history of the 1930s onwards which had led to a return 'of the primitive, garbled, war-time versions of the origins of the war of 1914'.[3] Their mistake, in Taylor's view, was to have relied too heavily on the German documents published in the *Grosse Politik,* which he knew from careful study to have been 'dangerously misleading, sometimes deliberately'. In his brief reply Butterfield wrote, as quoted near the beginning of this book, 'I am as a historian against all governments', consciously or unconsciously employing exactly the same words as Taylor had used of himself. Yet his

---

[1] Those who replied included G.R. Potter, J.E. Neale, T.S.R. Boase, Ernest Barker, Veronica Wedgwood, R.F. Treharne and J.R.M. Butler. He also received two letters from F.W. Crick of the *Contemporary Review,* to whom he had not sent an offprint.

[2] Taylor to Butterfield, 28 July 1949, BUTT/130/4. For details of the *TLS* affair, see the references on p. 4, note 21.

[3] *Studies,* p. 132; *Human Relations,* p. 189. This was a view Butterfield had maintained for some time: see his 'Tendencies in historical study in England', *Irish Historical Studies,* iv (Mar. 1945), 209–23 (pp. 215–16).

correspondence with Woodward and Medlicott shows that he was in fact a less implacable opponent.

Woodward wrote two long letters to Butterfield, both verging on the illegible, with many afterthoughts squeezed between lines or in the margins.[4] Both were frank and friendly; both contained a strong defence of his editorship of the British diplomatic documents on impeccably honest and pragmatic grounds.[5] There was, he wrote, one thing he always had in mind:

> This thing is that *all* the archives will be open some time or other, and any omissions, etc wld be disclosed to students & cld therefore reflect v. badly on the honesty of the editors. I don't want to get the posthumous reputation of a faker of history, & for this reason alone – apart from my own habits & training, I am likely to be careful![6]

He went on to stress the editorial independence and lack of official interference that he and Butler enjoyed:

> We have access to everything (we have also often asked the Cab. Office & No. 10 for papers wh. we thought might exist but for some reason were missing from the F.O. archives & we have never had any refusal) – including the private files of the Sec. of State wh. contain, mostly, personal letters (& some telegrams kept specially secret at the time – v. few of these are 'specially secret' now). We had to argue at first (this for your private information) about these personal letters – the question was whether they did or did not count as F.O. archives. We said they did, & we had our way. (I sometimes wonder whether Temperley saw as much – qualitatively – as we are seeing.)

Indeed it was Woodward who had come up with the publication programme and pressed it on the Foreign Office, not the other way round; and after some difficulty – with politicians, not officials – had it accepted:

> Eden was v. gd. about it – in insisting that there must be no 'monkeying' – Bevin has never shown any interest in the publication – at least he has never enquired about it – tho' I'm told that he is in fact interested in it.

Nor was there official interference in the selection of documents: the main difficulty, in fact, was in getting busy officials to read them once they had

---

[4] Butterfield had the second letter transcribed, presumably by his faithful secretary Eve Bogle. I have transcribed the first: it runs to around 1600 words.

[5] Butterfield told Medlicott that Woodward had earlier, in addition to these two letters, explained the situation 'in long conversations that I had had with him': letter of 5 August 1949, BUTT/130/4.

[6] Woodward to Butterfield, 28 July 1949, BUTT/130/4. All further references in this and the following two paragraphs are to this letter.

been prepared for publication. The editors were clear that they, and not the Foreign Office, had the last word:

> In fact, the F.O. comments are very few: they have never asked us to take out a document. (I've tried to stretch my memory, & I can't remember any such request – in fact F.O. influence or pressure is not a thing I have to bother about – I know we never have taken anything out.)

He added, however, that the Foreign Office had called attention to a few personal references that might 'cause offence to living people outside this country'; but '*In every case* – and there are not many cases – where we have cut anything out, we have put a footnote to this effect.'

The Foreign Office continued to insist on maintaining the practice of showing to foreign governments any documents emanating from them; but no government had refused so far. 'This is the question', Woodward recalled,

> on which Temperley had his great row, and my opinion – from reading these and other papers of T's exchanges with the FO is that T went about the whole thing in the wrong way … He was ridiculously bad-tempered, and the F.O. found him very trying, & to my mind were very patient and sensible with him.

Woodward had much more to say in his letter. He commented quite sharply on the content of Butterfield's article which, he said, lumped together

> (a) stuff emanating from the M[inistry] of I[nformation] during the war (b) official war histories (c) publication of documents such as my collection. (a) may be anything – and never claims to be objective history (b) has very different problems from (c).

He then went on to discuss his row with Taylor (about which he remained bitter), gave more explanation of the principles behind his selection of documents, and finally thanked Butterfield for his 'kindness – wh. I do appreciate in spite of my argufying – in sending it to me'.

Butterfield's reply to Woodward was convoluted and bordered on the obsequious at times; but it did help to clarify the intentions behind his article.[7] 'What I really had in mind', he wrote, 'was the relation of the State to history'. He had deliberately drawn his 'examples indiscriminately, with the effect of jumbling together things whose separate nature from a different point of view I am aware of'. His concern was

> the primacy of absolutely independent academic history, and I think sometimes that you will not realise the extraordinary power both of your position and the

---

[7] Butterfield to Woodward, 31 July 1949, BUTT/130/4.

State's and the fact that it would lead to a terrible situation if we did not regard you as a person to be shot at, indeed if we did not take care to keep the situation fluid.

Butterfield acknowledged the need for official history and did not doubt the honesty of Woodward and his colleagues; but, he said, there was always the possibility that they might make 'half-conscious slips'. And, as quoted earlier, he believed that the case of the German documents showed that the Foreign Office might trust some editors less than others, with the implication that they would not enjoy such a free hand. There followed a tortuous discussion of the Foreign Office's attitude to the control of information in which, despite all his circumlocutions, Butterfield got to the heart of the problem of official history. For the official historian possesses a privileged access denied to others: we have to take what he or she says on trust. Woodward was an honest man, Butterfield acknowledged, but others might be less honest. Official history must therefore always fall short of academic history because it is impossible to check all its sources:

> Official history cannot be judged by the methods adopted in all other kinds of history, that is to say by the direct reference to the totality of the sources, and if you were to say that it must be accepted on the personal credit of the historian, I know there is something in that, but I could not accept the view absolutely because in any age any scoundrel might make the claim, and it would be impossible for anybody to answer it, and in any case it does not allow for the fact that all historians sometimes get taken in by something.

Woodward's second letter was less defensive and contained insights that any subsequent editor of the British documents would recognize. He drew a distinction between narrative official histories and the publication of official documents.[8] As well as being editor of DBFP, Woodward was writing a history of British foreign policy during the Second World War.[9] Here he took the line that, 'on the basis of *all* the material', he was 'free to write as I please'; that the Cabinet Office and Foreign Office were free to decide whether to publish what he had written; and that if they did so they must publish it all without alteration. The only constraint was that of 'revealing Cabinet discussions & differences of opinion, while the people concerned are alive & active', bearing in mind the need to maintain Cabinet responsibility. Publishing Foreign Office documents was a different matter. Woodward thought that there was 'a line to be drawn between the record of the execution of policy, & the record of the formulation of policy', although

[8] Woodward to Butterfield, 1 August 1949, BUTT/130/4.
[9] See p. 47 below.

he admitted that it was blurred. But this very fact meant that in 'giving an account of what Br. Policy was & how it was carried out' (for example in volume I of series I) he was really giving 'a great deal of information abt. the formulation of naval policy, & later vols. even more abt. our policy on reparations & German claims'.

To publish more documents on the actual formulation of policy would run up against the problem of scale – a problem greater than anything faced by Gooch and Temperley. No account would be complete without the inclusion of Cabinet minutes, which had not been kept before the First World War. As for Foreign Office minutes, there had been many fewer before the war but then 'the top people wrote more', while 'they now write v. little & most of it is executive stuff, not statements of opinion'.[10] There was also the problem of content. Although the Foreign Office had not been asked explicitly for permission to publish *all* their policy-making stuff', Woodward thought that they would, if challenged, say no,

> & they would point out that the minutes are – & shld be – just 'first impressions' often provocatively written to start a line of enquiry – often framed in terms wh. if published wld give the deepest personal offence. (The F.O. type of humour wld often read v. offensively in print.) They wld claim that a man ought not to be pinned down in print to these miscellaneous jottings, wh. don't give *all* his ideas, & are merely tentative reactions (the same applies mutatis mutandis to many memoranda). I think this argument is one wh. a scientific historian must take into account.

As for the German documents,

> I don't think you need worry abt the selection of material in the German series, the intention is alright, and any mistakes & omissions will be due to the extreme difficulty of finding the material – the editors are explaining this.

Here, as we have seen, Woodward may have been economical with the truth.[11]

Norton Medlicott, as forthcoming as Woodward but unbruised by encounters with hostile reviewers, offered a more measured response to Butterfield's arguments (helped, perhaps, by the fact that his letters were typed rather than handwritten), and he undermined most of them by the application of relentless common sense and good humour. In his first letter

---

[10] This was a point echoed by Medlicott when he wrote to the *Times Literary Supplement* in defence of Woodward and Butler against a further criticism by Taylor: letter to *TLS*, 30 April 1949, p. 281.

[11] I have found no reply to Woodward's second letter in Butterfield's papers.

Medlicott challenged Butterfield's reference to 'motives of *raison d'état*, the public advantage, secret drawers, and then (in case we protest that we are not conscious that things are being withheld) the gullibility of official historians, lulled to sleep by the soft charms of officialdom':

> Really, it isn't like that at all. I have been an official historian alas since February 1942, writing the 'official' history of Economic Warfare during World War II ... I have had access to everything. Including the Cabinet Minutes. I have never been told that there is one drawer which I mustn't see ... it is no use saying that I am lulled by soft charms or bound with subtle chains because I simply have had the run of the whole place. All documents are filed in the Ministry's archives and registeries [*sic*], and I can either send for a file, or, if I like, go into the registry and get the stuff down for myself.[12]

Medlicott dated 'these constant suspicions of official hanky-panky' to the last era when diplomacy really had been secret, before the First World War. Since 1919, however, there had been 'Broadly speaking ... no secrets':

> Open diplomacy in its full horrors burst on us with Hitler and Mussolini, and our own diplomacy on all the major issues was public enough – Munich, discreditable or otherwise, was conducted in an awful blaze of publicity. And the real point about Woodward's documents – and the reason why they seem disappointing – is that on any matter that is really interesting – i.e. that was a matter of public interest at the time – we already know the worst (or best). Only the other day Woodward wrote to me and mentioned that I should find nothing of interest in his new volume on Munich, but that there would be some interesting things in Butler's forthcoming volume on 1919 and 1920 – Von der Goltz's activities in the Baltic etc! These were not of sufficient interest to attract contemporary historians at the time, and are therefore still a little novel.

Turning to the publication of minutes, Medlicott repeated many of the points Woodward had made, reinforcing them with his own experience of reading the 'pages of notes and speculations and arguments' that accompanied every telegram that arrived in the office, at the end of which 'something begins to emerge, and the official who is responsible for sending off a reply generally tells the man who has been smart enough to say something sensible, "please draft tel. on lines above" or words to that effect'. He agreed that 'from going through all this stuff you learn a great deal ... but it is also very tedious and often silly, and you must have some short cuts'. It would simply not be practicable to publish everything, and 'the real problem of all historical study after say 1800 is to wade through the endless

---

[12] Medlicott to Butterfield, 3 August 1949, BUTT/130/4. The two volumes of Medlicott's *The Economic Blockade* were published in 1952 and 1959.

masses of paper – particularly is this true in diplomacy. I don't want any more paper thrust on me in the job I am on now – I want on the other hand some machinery for sorting it all out.'

Medlicott ended with a strong defence of Woodward's editorial work:

> Really, I think someone ought to thank him and the FO for getting the stuff out. The real reason for publication after all is not to deceive the public, but to disarm criticism by putting all cards on the table. This is compatible with complete honesty in the editing.

In his reply to Medlicott, Butterfield refused to yield on what he regarded as the key point.[13] Woodward's work was important but it did not tell the whole story. That story could not be fully understood 'without studying the policy-making material'. None of the materials provided so far would provide insight into, for example, the part played by Vansittart in the making of British foreign policy before the Second World War. Nor did the available documents reveal 'the maximum of the offers we made to Russia in 1939'. Butterfield accepted that such material might 'be not easily publishable yet, but when I am presented with the case that we made these offers to Russia because we expected them to be rejected, I want the kind of materials that will enable me to answer that question'. He repeated that it was 'not really a question of honesty or dishonesty that is in question, though from what I can judge there is a seamy side to all government [that phrase again!], and it lies precisely at the lower level I want to get at'. And again Butterfield reiterated his warning that, although the present generation of historians might be honest, 'the next generation will be liable not to be'.

Medlicott's response again challenged one of Butterfield's central premises.[14] Even when archives were fully open, whether public or private, they never contained 'all' the documents, and all those who used the archives understood that fact, either explicitly or implicitly.

> The FO material in the PRO is not complete – one finds there only what the FO chooses to send (not secret service stuff for instance). This is a very different thing from having the run of the actual archives, as I am doing for example. This is one reason why I stick to the strange view that concealment in the secret drawer sense is not the real issue.

The main reason why archives were not open (apart from the convention that one must not publish documents about negotiations with foreign

13 Butterfield to Medlicott, 5 August 1949, BUTT/130/4.
14 Medlicott to Butterfield, 13 August 1949, BUTT/130/4.

governments without their consent) was not to conceal discreditable truths but to preserve the anonymity of public servants. 'When we say that the FO archives are open down to 1902 we mean of course that the government feels that the anonymity rule need not apply any longer before that date – not that everything is available.'

Medlicott went on to challenge another of Butterfield's cherished beliefs: the editorial independence of Gooch and Temperley. As far as he could see, they had been on exactly the same footing as Woodward and Butler: '"outside" historians, not members of the permanent FO staff'.

> Is there any difference? Woodward of course receives a salary. I don't know whether G. & T. did. It is not, however, a material point. Did they come under the Official Secrets Act? Woodward and myself and others do in the sense that we see everything, and obviously can't just rush out and publish anything snappy that we come across in the Evening News. But I don't imagine Temperley could either. The weapon we hold is that if permission to publish is withheld for what we think the wrong reasons we can resign and make a public protest.

He concluded: 'Of course there is a further point which we tend to forget – that the really vital ideas are often not put on paper at all, because they emerge in conversation between the head men.'[15]

Medlicott urged Butterfield not to bother to reply, and he evidently took him at his word. By the middle of August 1949 letters of thanks for his *Studies* article had dried up. Having asked the editor at the end of July for thirty extra offprints, 'as the article has brought to light attempts to prevent the publication here of criticisms of official history', he wrote to the printers a month later that 'the time has rather passed for circulating my article on Official History any further, so I have decided not to ask for any more off-prints now'.[16] By October Butterfield had changed his mind again and was asking for ten copies of the June 1949 issue of *Studies*, though there is no indication whether they were sent or received.[17] Could this renewed interest have been connected with an article by Desmond Williams on 'Some

---

[15] This was a point echoed by Butterfield's Cambridge colleague J.R.M. Butler, the editor-in-chief of the military series of the Cabinet Office's official histories programme, in a letter of thanks for a copy of *History and Human Relations* (he called it *Christianity and Human Relations*, an understandable mistake): '... one can never hope to describe all the circumstances of the conception and growth of a policy: so much is likely to have been done in conversation or even by a look': Butler to Butterfield, 12 August 1951, BUTT/130/4.

[16] Butterfield to Connolly, 25 July 1949, and to Messrs Alex. Thom & Co. Ltd, 24 August 1949, BUTT/130/4.

[17] Butterfield's secretary (Eve Bogle) to Educational Co. of Ireland Ltd, 12 October 1949, BUTT/130/4.

aspects of contemporary history' that appeared in the *Cambridge Journal* in September?[18] Published on the eve of taking up his professorship in Dublin, Williams's article had much in common with Butterfield's, notably in deprecating the willingness of modern historians to

> lend themselves as editors of 'official' history, subject often to the censorship of a departmental chief. The severity of the censorship varies widely of course in different countries, but the principle is one which formerly would have been rejected out of hand by all historians.[19]

The difference, of course, lay in the fact that Williams spoke from direct experience, though no hint of that fact appeared in his article. Characteristically, the aspects that particularly disturbed him were those where German wartime documents and the recently published memoirs of Churchill and others shed a sinister light on Allied conduct during the war, and their efforts to suppress consideration of such conduct by the International Military Tribunal at Nuremberg. Butterfield took notes on the article, focusing on the subject to which he had been alerted by Halvdan Koht in 1941 and to which he and Williams were to return with zeal in the early 1950s: the suggestion that the German invasion of Norway in April 1940 had merely forestalled a British invasion that was already under way.[20]

By now Butterfield was about to take up his Princeton sabbatical, and it would not have been surprising if official history, along with other preoccupations, had fallen away under the stimulus of that bracing intellectual environment. Instead, Princeton allowed Butterfield to reflect further on the subject, since it was during this time that he conceived a plan for collecting together some of the pieces he had written since the war, including his *Studies* article, in the volume that became *History and Human Relations* in 1951.[21] But reflection did not mean that Butterfield had modified his opinions in the light of the reassuring arguments of Woodward and Medlicott. If anything, they had been reinforced.

The perihelion of Mercury

So far, we have seen Butterfield's views as mediated by the criticism of other historians. It is time to look directly at the two versions of his article and to work out what he thought the criteria and pitfalls of official history actually

---

[18] *Cambridge Journal*, ii (Sept. 1949), 733–42.
[19] Ibid., p. 736.
[20] Undated record card with handwritten notes, BUTT/130/4.
[21] Bentley, *Butterfield*, p. 251.

were. Let us start with a passage already partially quoted:

> If I may be allowed to give what at least is not an unconsidered opinion, I must say that I do not personally believe that there is a government in Europe which wants the public to know all the truth.[22]

The sentence is typical Butterfield: starting diffidently and with one of his habitual double negatives, it ends with a memorable punchline. We have already seen many indications of Butterfield's scepticism towards government and its efforts to manage the past. To what extent, if at all, did his views change between the two versions of his article published in 1949 and 1951?

First, however, we need to look back to his early intellectual development under the tutelage of Harold Temperley: for it was in this period, according to Michael Bentley, that his scepticism was rooted. For Butterfield, expressions of filial piety towards Temperley were routine, usually coupled with disparaging comments on Temperley's long-standing rival, Charles Webster. In 1943, for example, he lamented to a visiting Norwegian historian the

> lack of first-rank historians in England at the moment, at least as far as modern history was concerned. There was no one who could replace Temperley. Webster was perhaps the best known. He was a diligent historian but Butterfield thought he was secondrate. His historical work relied too exclusively on diplomatic documents and lacked back-ground.[23]

Yet Bentley makes a persuasive case that Butterfield's scepticism was directed towards Temperley just as much as towards official history. On arriving at Peterhouse in 1919, Butterfield's first encounter with Temperley had gone very badly. It was only Paul Vellacott's kindness that rescued his undergraduate career – and it was only after reading one of his first essays that Temperley started to take serious notice of him. Temperley then became 'a dominant force in his undergraduate life' and later his postgraduate supervisor. But, in Bentley's view, it is too easy to assume that Butterfield owed everything to Temperley's teaching 'and had his mind formed in Temperley's mould', for this ignores the fact 'that Butterfield was very clever indeed and that Temperley was not'. In notes for the biography that he could never bring himself to write, Butterfield wrote that Temperley had 'the heart of a child'.

---

[22] *Studies*, p. 130; *Human Relations*, p. 186.

[23] *Arne Ordings dagbøker*, vol. I, *19. juni 1942–23. juli 1945*, ed. Erik Opsahl (Oslo, 2000), pp. 155–6 (entry for 27 February 1943): my translation. The words 'secondrate' and 'background' are given in English in the original.

He was a 'boisterous schoolboy', 'a sentimentalist'.[24] Butterfield, Bentley writes, detected that 'Temperley's intellectual posturing had a hollow centre'.[25] Although unwilling to admit it publicly, he was equally sceptical of the kind of official history that Temperley was producing in his capacity as co-editor of the British documents, at the same time as he was supervising Butterfield's training as a diplomatic historian. As with the man so with the work: the nostalgia for the historians of the late 1920s that Butterfield expressed when writing to Taylor is deceptive. Convinced that history was worth studying only for its own sake, not for its imagined usefulness to civic life, Butterfield reacted against the 'new' diplomatic history as practised by Temperley and, especially, Webster, with its claim to learn 'lessons' from the Congress of Vienna that could be applied to Versailles, the League of Nations and so on.[26] As he was to write much later, 'What you have to avoid in 1919 are not the mistakes of 1815 but the mistakes of 1919.'[27] By the time he had completed his first and only essay in the discipline, Butterfield had rejected diplomatic history itself. 'There is something in the history of diplomacy which inclines to be cold and forbidding, and lacks the full-blooded leap of the larger story of human lives,' he wrote in the conclusion to *The Peace Tactics of Napoleon, 1806–1809*, published in 1929.[28]

At the end of the war, Butterfield's belief in the absolute primacy of academic historical enquiry remained unshaken. He reacted indignantly to a proposal by the Air Ministry that research assistants working on the official history of the war in the air might be permitted to submit their work for research degrees at the universities of Oxford or Cambridge.[29] This, he thought, was just another example of 'the growing power (in these matters) of the state, which has been putting out its tentacles and tightening its grip upon us'.[30] Yet Butterfield accepted the use of history by government

---

[24] Quoted in Bentley, *Butterfield*, p. 42.

[25] Ibid.

[26] Ibid., p. 59.

[27] 'The dangers of history', in *History and Human Relations*, pp. 158–81 (pp. 176–7).

[28] Quoted in Bentley, *Butterfield*, p. 63. But 'he remained convinced that a piece of diplomatic history was as good a training as any for the young historian': John Derry, 'Herbert Butterfield', in *The Historian at Work*, ed. John Cannon (London, 1980), p. 180. That Butterfield also acknowledged the limitations of diplomatic history is shown in Jeremy Black and Karl Schweizer, 'The value of diplomatic history: A case study in the thought of Herbert Butterfield', *Diplomacy and Statecraft*, xvii (2006), 617–31.

[29] Grahame Clark to Butterfield, 3 February 1945, enclosing a draft Air Ministry memorandum, BUTT/130/1. For the background to this proposal, see Frankland, *History at War*, p. 38.

[30] Handwritten notes, 'Research degrees for work in government depts. etc.', 11 February 1945, p. 2, BUTT/130/1.

as long as it did not encroach on the academic sphere. He agreed with his Peterhouse colleague, the archaeologist Grahame Clark, then working for the Air Ministry, that it should be encouraged to 'establish an Historical Section, which should have its place in the elaboration of strategy, in Staff College training etc.' (and, incidentally, help to allay the Air Ministry's 'jealousy of the Admiralty', whose historical traditions were more firmly established).[31]

Butterfield's *Studies* article therefore drew upon deep-seated views about the nature of history and the role of the state, reinforced by evidence from the war and the immediate post-war period of a growing interest in history on the part of the British government which might ostensibly be well-meaning, but – as Desmond Williams had revealed – might serve more malign purposes. In his article Butterfield started by insisting that 'an independent science of history' was an essential component of freedom of thought. But it was in danger of being compromised when independent historians placed themselves at the service of government, however patriotic their motives.[32] Butterfield went on to express his belief that no government wanted the public to know all the truth – if it did, it had 'only to open its archive to the free play of scholarship' – and adumbrated two maxims that followed from such unwillingness. First was the existence of a 'secret drawer'. 'Governments', Butterfield claimed, 'try to press upon the historian the keys to all the drawers but one, and are very anxious to spread the belief that this single one contains no secret of importance.' 'Secondly,' he went on, 'if the historian can only find out the thing which government does not want him to know, he will lay his hand upon something that is likely to be significant.'[33]

The secret drawer was a conviction from which Butterfield never wavered: Medlicott's good-humoured denial of its existence made no impression. Interestingly, Medlicott quoted Butterfield on the subject in his inaugural lecture as Stevenson Professor of International History at LSE in 1955. He also quoted Lord Acton's claim that 'one key is always excepted'; and suggested that Acton, a historian who preoccupied Butterfield for the whole of his

[31] Ibid., pp. 2, 4. If Butterfield's objections had been accepted, they would have thwarted the ambitions of Noble Frankland, who was to become one of the most distinguished of all official historians (see pp. 46–7 below). Frankland was admitted to read for a DPhil at Oxford in January 1949 (Woodward was one of the faculty members who accepted his proposal); his thesis on the history of the strategic bombing offensive was awarded in April 1951: see Frankland, *History at War*, pp. 38, 57.

[32] *Studies*, p. 130; *Human Relations*, p. 185.

[33] *Studies*, p. 130; *Human Relations*, p. 186.

working life, might have been the source of his belief.[34] Yet the instances in which Butterfield claimed to detect the phenomenon were startlingly few. Indeed there is only one clear example in international affairs, cited in both versions of his official history article and discussed at greater length in the lectures that became *Man on His Past* in 1955: the claim by Frederick the Great in 1756 that he had opened the Seven Years' War on discovering a dangerous conspiracy against him on the part of Austria and Russia.[35] It was only when the Russian archives were opened, as late as 1912, that the conspiracy was proved to have been 'more dangerous than Frederick ever knew': 'Only when the last drawer was unlocked did we discover that what required to be explained was a certain gullibility that Frederick had shown in the period when the conspiracy was being developed.'[36]

In the main body of his article Butterfield developed the arguments that, as we have seen, provoked the most dissent from Woodward and Medlicott: that Gooch and Temperley had held 'a peculiarly independent position' as editors of the *British Documents*; that the dispassionate historiography of the 1920s had been supplanted by ideologically driven interpretations of the war's origin; that the Second World War had witnessed an intensified race by governments to state their case through official histories or the publication of official documents; and that the post-war editing of German and British documents by nominally independent historians fell short of the high standard set by their British predecessors after the First World War. The problem, Butterfield went on, was that the outside reader had no way of knowing 'the machinery or the series of processes' through which documents were selected and who, other than historians, had a say in that selection.[37]

This was a point amplified in the version of the article published in *History and Human Relations* in 1951. 'It would even be useful', Butterfield wrote in a new sentence, 'if all the rules governing the work of official historians could be published; since it is conceivable, for example, that regulations restricting certain powers or privileges to a chief editor would raise an

---

[34] W.N. Medlicott, 'The scope and study of international history', *International Affairs*, xxxi (1955), 413–26 (p. 419).

[35] A similar example from domestic affairs, cited in the later version of the article and elsewhere, was that of a recently discovered letter from Charles James Fox showing that he was privately less keen on parliamentary reform in 1792 than he claimed to be in public: *Human Relations*, p. 208.

[36] *Studies*, p. 139; *Human Relations*, pp. 209–10; 'The reconstruction of an historical episode: The history of the enquiry into the origins of the Seven Years War', in Herbert Butterfield, *Man on His Past: The Study of the History of Historical Scholarship* (Cambridge, 1955), pp. 143–70.

[37] *Studies*, p. 136.

issue of some significance.'[38] The later version also elaborated Butterfield's suggestion that official historians practised what we would now term self-censorship. It would be a mistake, Butterfield claimed in another addition to the original text, to imagine that modern governments needed to rely on direct censorship to ensure that their version of the truth reached the public.

Old-fashioned censorship had been

> transformed into the phenomenon of 'auto-censorship' – a matter to be borne in mind even when the people involved are only indirectly the servants of government, or are attached by no further tie than the enjoyment of privileges that might be taken away.[39]

Might we read these additions as an implicit rejoinder to Woodward and Medlicott?

The 1951 version also showed that Butterfield remained unpersuaded by Woodward's justification for the exclusion of Foreign Office minutes from *Documents on British Foreign Policy*. On the contrary, he elaborated his argument that such minutes were essential to understanding 'the history of the way in which British foreign policy came to be arrived at and formulated'.[40] He admitted that there might be good reasons for not publishing policy-making material so soon after the events in question; but their absence must arouse the suspicion that 'officialdom' had reasons for not wanting it to be published. Here again, Butterfield came in his roundabout way to the heart of the matter. For he believed that it was only through access to such material that it was possible to identify the real makers of policy: not the Foreign Secretary but 'the higher permanent officials of the Foreign Office' (he was presumably thinking of figures like Vansittart) who, if they could not 'force their policy on a Foreign Secretary', were at any rate 'strong enough to prevent him from carrying out any other policy of his own':[41]

> It is the people most responsible for the real development of our foreign policy – though they may not be technically responsible to Parliament – who gain remarkable cover from the decision to exclude that material in the case of the English series. These sub-governmental, sub-ministerial actors in the drama are bound to be the real objective of a genuine enquiry into British foreign policy; and the real secrets – indeed the real problems in some of our minds

---

[38] *Human Relations*, p. 197.
[39] Ibid., p. 197.
[40] Ibid., p. 202.
[41] Ibid., p. 203.

– are situated in the very nature of things at this level. It does not require a knowledge of the materials that are withheld from us to enable us to see that the documents which are being published are insufficient for the genuine reconstruction of British foreign policy.[42]

The most substantial transformation of the original article came in a section that brought Butterfield's arguments together in a remarkable synthesis.[43] To show that we must always be prepared for some new fact 'which will challenge our inelasticities of mind and shake the validities of things we never thought to question',[44] Butterfield drew attention to some Foreign Office minutes from July 1914 in the published British documents which might never have been printed and, in that case, 'would hardly have been missed', but which cast an entirely new light on British preoccupations. For what they showed was that in 1914 senior officials were at least as worried about Russia as about Germany, perhaps more so. Butterfield also pointed to two omissions from the published documents, both relating to Russia, and noted that the introduction by Sir James Headlam-Morley, historical adviser to the Foreign Office, again sought to guide the reader to a particular view of 'the Russian side of the question'.[45] Fear of Russian power had been a nineteenth-century obsession, and was again an obsession in the early years of the Cold War. In that perspective, conflict with Germany was no more than a 'curious interlude of some thirty years from 1914'.[46] Inelasticity of mind, reinforced by the way in which the British documents had been edited after both world wars – what was included in the published volumes and what was not included – had led to a distorted view of Britain's international situation in the first half of the twentieth century. We must now ask ourselves, Butterfield wrote, 'whether for thirty years we have not construed our contemporary history within too narrow a framework':

> We may have been as virtuous as we assert, or at least we may have been well-intentioned, but both our historiography and our diplomacy may still be open to the charge of unimaginativeness if, while Germany and Russia have been alternate menaces of over a hundred years, we have failed to widen our vision – failed ever to think of more than one of these possible menaces at the same time, failed to envisage two possible enemies at once, failed even to see how far they could be made to act as a mutual check and thus cancel one another out to some degree.

[42] Ibid., pp. 204–5.
[43] Elements of the argument appear on pp. 138 and 139–41 of the *Studies* article.
[44] *Human Relations*, p. 210.
[45] Ibid., p. 215.
[46] Ibid., p. 212.

Such passages help to explain why A.J.P. Taylor felt able to lump Butterfield along with those in the United States and Great Britain who had advocated sitting tight while Germany and Russia fought each other to destruction.[47] In fact Butterfield was saying something much less crude. By favouring one 'monstrous ogre' over the other, Britain had contradicted one of the deepest principles of British foreign policy: that it should 'fight any single power that threatened to dominate the Continent', but not 'so to destroy one of the giants that half a continent was left at the good or bad intentions of the other'.[48] The mission to destroy Germany had been conducted so relentlessly through two world wars that it had left no space for 'the difficult obligation of keeping two areas of force in our survey at once, two dangers in mind at the same time', and the result had been the domination of half a continent by the Soviet Union.[49] And the danger of official history was that it would legitimate only one view of the course of events over the last thirty years – the 'Foreign Office view of history' – ignoring, suppressing or simply failing to notice evidence that might point to alternative interpretations.[50] All this was a long way beyond the dusty metaphor of the secret drawer, not to mention the minutiae of the Windsor papers; and to illuminate his point Butterfield drew on his new understanding of the history of science. In what Michael Bentley has described as 'a brilliant passage', Butterfield brought science and history together in an 'extraordinary metaphor':[51]

> A slight discrepancy in regard to the perihelion of Mercury – a discrepancy so small that it was not even measurable in the case of other planets – called for the radically new synthesis of Einstein to explain it and to embrace all the known elements in the case. In regard to a piece of history there are always many facets which are intractable whatever system we adopt, and there is always a chance that one of these may be our perihelion of Mercury.[52]

For Butterfield, it was precisely the fact that 'there were two things which people ought to have been thinking about at once' – Russia as well as Germany – that official history had concealed but which, once discovered, constituted 'the historian's perihelion of Mercury'.

---

[47] Review of Charles Tansill, *Back Door to War: Roosevelt's Foreign Policy 1933–1941*, *Manchester Guardian*, 24 October 1952, reprinted as 'Roosevelt and the war', in *Struggles for Supremacy*, ed. Wrigley, pp. 245–7.

[48] *Human Relations*, p. 217.

[49] Ibid., p. 214.

[50] Ibid., p. 223.

[51] Bentley, *Butterfield*, p. 202.

[52] *Human Relations*, pp. 210–11.

After 'Pitfalls'

Herbert Butterfield went on to greater things: Master of Peterhouse, President of the Historical Association, Vice-Chancellor of Cambridge University, Regius Professor of History at Cambridge, Fellow of the British Academy, a knighthood. *Christianity and History*, above all, made him an international celebrity: in Brendan Simms's words, 'Butterfield became something of a sage among many Christian intellectuals, a prophet even.'[53] Intellectually, his interests moved on to historiography and international relations. Many projects remained unfulfilled: he never wrote his history of diplomacy or his biographies of Temperley and Charles James Fox. In person, the Sage of Peterhouse was very different from his public reputation. As 'one who still remembers the famous Butterfield giggle', Geoffrey Elton recalled Butterfield with affection before going on to demolish much of his reputation as a historian:

> Those who knew only the voice, on paper at that, were liable to be profoundly disconcerted when they encountered him: no whitebearded old testament prophet after all, preaching stern simplicities, but a clean-shaven (often somewhat razored) man permanently about thirty-five years old, brisk, cheerful, responsive, entertaining, variously chain-smoking or sworn off cigarettes altogether, always courteous, never pompous.[54]

Maurice Cowling confirmed that 'after shaving, his face was often like a battlefield';[55] Ved Mehta, in his charming account of a lunch at the Master's Lodge, recorded the Player's cigarette that 'hung from his lower lip, and threatened to fall off at any moment'.[56] John Cannon, who knew Butterfield as an undergraduate at Peterhouse, summed him up with characteristic brevity:

> A small, alert man, with a gentle manner and shy charm, he was a gifted and vigorous lecturer, particularly on European history, with a penchant for lurid phraseology which occasionally spilled over into his printed work.[57]

[53] Brendan Simms, 'Butterfield, Sir Herbert (1900–1979)', *Oxford Dictionary of National Biography*, <https://doi.org/10.1093/ref:odnb/30888>.

[54] G.R. Elton, 'Herbert Butterfield and the study of history', *Historical Journal*, xxvii (1984), 729–43 (p. 729).

[55] Maurice Cowling, 'Herbert Butterfield, 1900–1979', *Proceedings of the British Academy*, lxv (1979), 595–609 (p. 607).

[56] Ved Mehta, *Fly and the Fly Bottle: Encounters with British Intellectuals* (London, 1961), p. 195.

[57] 'Butterfield, Herbert', in *The Blackwell Dictionary of Historians*, ed. John Cannon et al. (Oxford, 1988), p. 61.

Under Butterfield, Peterhouse became famous as the centre of what Noel Annan denounced as 'a kind of militant conservatism distinct from the Establishment conservatism of most Cambridge colleges. It was radical, reverent towards Christianity, irreverent towards liberals and scornful of socialists.'[58] It was also relentlessly negative. John Vincent recalled the other side of that famous giggle:

> The tendency at High Table was to reduce all issues to a shrill camp giggle, much mimicked – of high seriousness, whether northern or Methodist, nothing showed. This struck us, of course, as a version of greatness.[59]

Such behaviour persisted long after Butterfield's retirement in 1968. As a younger man an exceptionally considerate personal tutor,[60] as Master Butterfield could be remote and often intimidating with students. Ironically, perhaps, in view of his large and growing band of posthumous disciples, he established no 'school'.[61] But that was never his intention. 'The point of teaching history to undergraduates', he told Ved Mehta, 'is to turn them into future public servants and statesmen.'[62] Yet he continued to delight in subversion: in the words of Maurice Cowling's obituary, 'He rejected authority in historical thinking, attaching supreme importance to inventiveness, paradox, and interpretative deviance.' And, Cowling continues, 'He felt a deep and irrational regard for rakes whom he much preferred to the "virtuous and stiff-necked".'[63] Desmond Williams was one of those rakes. The two men met and corresponded for the rest of Butterfield's life. Williams wrote little but exerted his charm on generations of students at UCD. He was more successful than Butterfield in inspiring future scholars and more generous in fostering their future careers. He retired on grounds of ill health in 1983 and died in 1987, aged 66.

For a while, Butterfield continued to annoy the official historians. His name became a byword for carping criticism. In 1951 Woodward, by now a research professor at the Institute for Advanced Study at Princeton,

---

[58] Noel Annan, *Our Age: Portrait of a Generation* (London, 1990), p. 270.

[59] Quoted in Bentley, *Butterfield*, p. 285.

[60] John Cloake, 'The scholar cadet: More recollections of Peterhouse in the 1940s', *Peterhouse Annual Record 2003/2004*, pp. 13–25.

[61] Unless, of course, one counts the 'Peterhouse school of historians' that caused Hugh Trevor-Roper so much distress after he became Master of the College (as Lord Dacre) in 1980: see *One Hundred Letters from Hugh Trevor-Roper*, ed. Richard Davenport-Hines and Adam Sisman (Oxford, 2014), p. 254 (where Dacre holds Butterfield largely to blame) and especially pp. 273–6.

[62] Mehta, *Fly and the Flybottle*, p. 196.

[63] Cowling, 'Herbert Butterfield', p. 608.

wrote to Margaret Lambert commiserating with her on the lack of support for modern documentary publishing on the part of the Royal Historical Society:

> The thing is that – even now – people who are doing very difficult documentary work on very modern material are – in this country – doing something *new*, and must not expect 'recognition' though it is a little hard that they shld get so many kicks from the Butterfields.[64]

In 1953 Rohan Butler wrote:

> I find that sometimes suspicious questioners, who either doubt or have not bothered to read the assurances as to full freedom given in all our prefaces, ask me exactly what files we are allowed to see. (I had considerable difficulty in persuading one foreign gentleman that all the most important files were not withheld from us, and even Butterfield seems inclined to cherish the same ridiculous idea.)[65]

They also responded publicly to Butterfield's criticisms: implicitly in Woodward's Raleigh Lecture to the British Academy in 1950; humorously in Hancock's Webb Memorial Lecture of the same year; explicitly, as we have seen, in Medlicott's inaugural lecture at LSE in 1955.[66]

Butterfield's official history file thins out after 1951 and I have discovered no further references to the subject in print. The clearest expression of what he was trying to say appears, typically, not in any published work but in a letter of May 1952 to a South African clergyman who had read *History and Human Relations* and was worried about the intention of the National Party government to use official history to legitimize the antecedents of the apartheid state.[67] In just over three closely typed pages, Butterfield set out his views with unprecedented concision, including what was perhaps his core belief: 'I am sure that on a long-term view the ideal thing for historical study is a world of independent historians, choosing their own subjects for research, and allowed by the government free access to the archives.'[68] Then, after an interval of nearly thirty years, we find the letter I quoted near the

---

[64] Woodward to Lambert, 26/27 September 1951, Lambert papers.

[65] 'Additional notes for a talk on F.O. Library and publications' (by Woodward), 6 January 1953, FCO Historians' collection.

[66] E.L. Woodward, 'Some considerations on the present state of historical studies' (read 17 May 1950), *Proceedings of the British Academy 1950*, pp. 95–112; Hancock quoted in Harris, 'Thucydides amongst the mandarins', p. 135; Medlicott, 'International history', p. 419.

[67] Rev. A.W. Blaxall to Butterfield, 6 April 1952, BUTT/130/4.

[68] Butterfield to Blaxall, 9 May 1952, BUTT/130/4. The correspondence with Rev. Blaxall is reproduced in full as an appendix to this book (see Appendix I).

beginning of this book, written to Desmond Williams a year before his death in 1979, in which he counselled historians to steer clear of government patronage. Butterfield continued:

> I think I probably touched on some aspects of this in the paper on *Official History* which I gave somewhere in Dublin soon after the Second World War, and which appeared at that time in *Studies*, and which I understand is being reprinted in the US after being used at a Conference which I didn't attend.[69]

By now the memory was hazy, but the conviction remained undimmed.

[69] Butterfield to Williams, 3 May 1978 (unsigned draft), BUTT/531/W/385. See the comment on p. 4, note 14.

3. Official history then and now

Precisely at the point at which Butterfield lost interest in the subject, official history in the United Kingdom came into its own. It is hard now to recollect that until the thirty-year rule came into effect in 1969, official narrative histories and collections of diplomatic documents were virtually the only available sources for the inner workings of government in the first half of the twentieth century. No wonder, therefore, that Namier and Taylor fell upon successive volumes of DBFP and DGFP so avidly: beyond memoirs, biographies and published diaries, they were all they had.[1] No wonder, too, that Taylor had to rely so heavily on the official histories of the two world wars when writing his *English History 1914–1945*, while challenging the basic premise of official history in terms almost identical to Butterfield's:

> All these volumes rest on a contradiction. If, as their authors and editors claim, they reveal everything essential, nothing remains to conceal, and the archives could be opened without harm to all. If, on the other hand, there are still secrets, the authors and editors have not kept their promise to the public. The unofficial historian can only register his protest and repeat with Charles A. Beard: 'Official archives must be open to all citizens on equal terms, with special privileges for none.'[2]

The civil and military histories of the Second World War

Whatever their limitations, the official histories were indispensable. In terms of sheer output, Hancock's civil and Butler's military series represented a formidable achievement. In the late 1940s and 1950s alone, more than forty volumes were published, followed by a further twenty volumes in

[1] Admittedly Namier tended to prefer memoirs and diaries to diplomatic documents. But see his *Diplomatic Prelude 1938–1939* (London, 1948) for a formidable early analysis based on the 'coloured books' published by the British, French, Polish and German governments following the outbreak of war; and *Europe in Decay 1936–1940* (London, 1950), for his use of DBFP and DGFP, as well as *Nazi-Soviet Relations, 1939–1941* and documents published by the Soviet Union. For Taylor, see the reviews collected in *Struggles for Supremacy*, ed. Wrigley, passim. The two series also account for the overwhelming majority of the references in Taylor's *The Origins of the Second World War* (London, 1961).

[2] A.J.P. Taylor, *English History 1914–1945* (Oxford, 1965), quoted from the revised paperback edition (Harmondsworth, 1970), p. 731.

the following decade.[3] While some were undistinguished, others, as Taylor tersely acknowledged, were works of lasting quality. They included Richard Titmuss's *Problems of Social Policy* (1950), 'a remarkable essay in creative understanding'; T.K. Derry's *The Campaign in Norway* (1952), 'remarkably frank'; and *The Strategic Air Offensive against Germany* (1961) by Temperley's old sparring partner (and Butterfield's *bête-noire*) Sir Charles Webster and Noble Frankland (who had served in Bomber Command during the war), 'the most ruthlessly impartial of all official histories'.[4]

Yet Butterfield would have found much to reinforce his suspicions in the battles fought behind the scenes between authors and editors on the one hand and officialdom on the other. Even Hancock, who had prided himself on his ability to forge a 'creative partnership' between historians and officials, became disillusioned when draft copies of *British War Economy*, circulated in 1947, 'evoked an instant torrent of official criticism and complaint'.[5] Hancock had insisted that 'the histories must be critical. To have told a "success story" – even when the success had been in the end resplendent – would have been futile and dangerous; the main processes of trial and error had to be revealed.'[6] But such frankness was exactly what civil servants objected to. They did not wish policy to be shown as the product of 'internecine warfare' or 'muddle, improvisation and fortuitous decisions'.[7] Perhaps worn down by their objections, Hancock accepted most of the changes required.[8] 'The result', Jose Harris writes, 'was that the published edition of *British War Economy* was a much greyer, more discreet, more anonymous and less popularly accessible work than the original draft version.'[9] The obstacles faced by Webster and Frankland were still greater, for their dissection of the strategy underpinning Bomber Command's campaign of area bombing challenged not only the success of that campaign but the very doctrine upon which the Royal Air Force had

---

[3] For lists of the civil and military series, see Appendix II below. With a few exceptions published in the 1980s, all of the official narrative histories, as well as DBFP and DGFP, were published by Her Majesty's Stationery Office, London, until the privatization of HMSO in 1996.

[4] Taylor, *English History*, pp. 762–3.

[5] Harris, 'Thucydides amongst the mandarins', p. 136.

[6] W.K. Hancock and M.M. Gowing, *British War Economy* (London, 1949), p. xi. The complete volume is available at <http://www.ibiblio.org/hyperwar/UN/UK/UK-Civil-WarEcon/index.html>.

[7] Quoted in Harris, 'Thucydides amongst the mandarins', p. 136.

[8] In his memoirs, *Country and Calling* (London, 1954), pp. 203–4, Hancock gives a more positive account.

[9] Harris, 'Thucydides amongst the mandarins', p. 139.

been founded in 1918.[10] In the face of opposition from wartime leaders as eminent as Viscount Portal and Sir Arthur Harris, it eventually required the intervention of the Cabinet Secretary, Sir Norman Brook, to secure approval for publication by the Prime Minister, Harold Macmillan.[11] After such ordeals it was unlikely that any official historian, even one whose work had achieved publication relatively unscathed, would have felt touched by the subtle 'influence upon historians of admission to the charmed circle'.[12]

Documents on British Foreign Policy 1919–1939

The publication of *Documents on British Foreign Policy 1919–1939* proceeded at a steady pace and with little further controversy. The third series, covering the 1938–9 period, was completed in nine volumes between 1949 and 1955. The fact that they were published so soon after the events they recorded seems remarkable by today's standards (it is as if we were now publishing documents from the early years of the Cameron administration) and helped to compensate for the prolonged closure of the official archives. The first and second series, together with a new series IA (covering the period 1925–30), inevitably took much longer to complete. Woodward retired as editor in 1958, but DBFP continued under the editorship of Rohan Butler, Patrick Bury, Douglas Dakin, Margaret Lambert[13] and Norton Medlicott, to be concluded in 1984 in a total of sixty-four volumes.[14] However, the publication of Woodward's narrative history of *British Foreign Policy in the Second World War*, completed in 1956, proved far more problematic and deeply frustrating for the ageing author. An abridged edition was published in 1962; the full five volumes did not appear until the early 1970s, by which time the documents to which they referred were already open at the Public Record Office.[15]

DBFP did not entirely escape criticism. Writing ten years after the

[10] Frankland, *History at War*, pp. 80–113, gives an intense personal account, reinforced by archive sources; Seb Cox, 'Setting the historical agenda: Webster and Frankland and the debate over the strategic bombing offensive against Germany, 1939–1945', in *The Last Word: Essays on Official History in the United States and the British Commonwealth*, ed. Jeffrey Grey (Westport, CT, and London, 2003), pp. 147–73, provides important context and perspective.

[11] Ibid., pp. 158–9. Webster died seven weeks before the volumes were published, leaving Frankland alone to face the controversy that blew up in the press.

[12] *Studies*, p. 136; *Human Relations*, p. 198.

[13] Later Margaret Pelly: no relation to the Hon. Margaret Lambert.

[14] For a complete list see Appendix IV below.

[15] Sir Llewellyn Woodward, *British Foreign Policy in the Second World War* (5 vols, London, 1970–6). For the full story see Beck, 'Locked in a dusty cupboard'. Dying in 1971, Woodward survived to see only the first volume in print.

end of the war, Desmond Williams returned to a familiar theme.[16] He acknowledged that later volumes in the third series published some internal Foreign Office minutes but complained that they were mostly confined to the footnotes. This suggested that 'the editors may have had a "guilty conscience". Otherwise why should they have reversed their original decision, and then only do so in half-hearted fashion?' He also complained about the privileged access granted to official historians – who must be 'people in whom the Foreign Office has special confidence' – but denied to others.[17] Having got these gripes out of the way, Williams made some serious points. He compared DBFP unfavourably with DGFP because the latter (as he knew well) drew on a much wider range of official German sources, not least the Führer Chancellery, and thus gave a much clearer understanding of German policy. More importantly, and very much in the spirit of Butterfield's 'Foreign Office view of history', he argued that there was 'a fundamental defect in that the editors seem to have been working within a limited framework of ideas'.[18] It was a 'framework of the anti-appeasement viewpoint' in which the documents selected by the editors seemed designed to ensure that the Foreign Office came out well.[19] Because these documents were the only ones available to the reader, it was impossible to discover the full range of options and calculations in the minds of officials and ministers at the time:

> One is entitled to inquire if any such evidence was available, and if it was rejected for publication by Mr Woodward and Mr Butler as being irrelevant to the 'main issue'. It is certainly possible that the two distinguished editors were in fact working within a certain framework, and that what for them was the 'main issue' is not the only one with which subsequent historians of the period will be concerned.[20]

[16] T. Desmond Williams, 'The historiography of World War II', in *Historical Studies* I, ed. Williams (London, 1958), pp. 33–49; reprinted in *The Origins of the Second World War: Historical Interpretations*, ed. Esmonde M. Robertson (London and Basingstoke, 1971), pp. 36–64. The first sentence of the article makes clear that it was written in 1955.

[17] Ibid., p. 44.

[18] Ibid., pp. 45–6.

[19] Ibid., p. 46. This is, of course, the same argument as he had made about the selection of the German documents at the time he was working on them: see p. 10 above.

[20] Ibid., pp. 48–9. For an early analysis following the opening of the Foreign Office files, see Donald Lammers, 'From Whitehall after Munich: The Foreign Office and the future course of British policy', *Historical Journal*, xvi (1973), 831–56. In footnote 49 (pp. 853–4), Lammers writes: 'A preliminary survey of some of the relevant papers does, nonetheless, suggest pretty strongly that it may be easy to over-state the case for the existence within the diplomatic service of a deep and coherent opposition to the main lines of government policy.'

Many of Williams's points were repeated and amplified when Frank Spencer took stock of the state of play in 1962.[21] He was in agreement over 'the general superiority of the German over the British collection', but did not find evidence of 'tendentious selection', blaming instead the sheer mass of material with which the editors had to contend, as well as the pressure of time:

> Publication began before they had thoroughly surveyed the whole of the archive material; more editors were needed; and more time should have been taken over their work. This would have made possible both a greater degree of objective consistency ... and the even more obvious benefits afforded by reading all the available evidence before publishing the findings.[22]

Documents on German Foreign Policy 1918–1945

Spencer's main criticism concerned the fate of *Documents on German Foreign Policy 1918–1945*. The series had been, he reported, 'drastically curtailed'.[23] The American, British and French governments had decided not to publish the projected volumes on the Weimar period and to terminate the series not in May 1945 but in December 1941. This simplified a complicated story. By 1960 the captured documents had been returned to the care of the West German Foreign Office in Bonn and in 1961 the original tripartite editorial project had been extended to include German editors. Although the new quadripartite team would publish no further volumes in English translation, German-language volumes would cover the Weimar period in series A and B, while a new series E would cover the period from 1941 to the end of the war. These decisions represented the conclusion of a decade of wrangling between the federal German government and the governments of Britain, France and the United States. Much of the resistance to the return of the documents and the participation of German editors had been led by British historians.[24] In December 1953, the Foreign Office's Historical Advisory Committee, comprising Namier, Medlicott, Woodward and Wheeler-Bennett, came down strongly in support of the British editors' objections to such a move. Uppermost in their minds was not any suspicion of Nazi sympathies but the fear, once again, that the German Foreign Office might seek to influence access to the documents

---

[21] Spencer, 'The publication of British and German diplomatic documents'.

[22] Ibid., pp. 256, 259.

[23] Ibid., p. 255.

[24] George O. Kent, 'Editing diplomatic documents: A review of official US and German document series', *American Archivist*, lvii (1994), 462–81; Zala, *Geschichte*, pp. 242–3; Eckert, *Struggle for the Files*, pp. 315–32.

and their selection for publication, just as had happened with the *Grosse Politik* in the 1920s.[25] 'Guarantees are waste paper,' Namier wrote. 'Once the documents are back in Germany, the German archivists will have the whip hand.' 'The present German government', he went on, 'is in a spiritual line of descent from the Weimar Republic; and it is its story that they will be keenest to obfuscate.'[26] As Donald Watt observed, the episode illustrated 'the ferocious hostility towards Germany inherent in their generation of senior historians': a hostility that proved strong enough to delay the return of the archives for a further seven years despite the Foreign Office's desire to conciliate a government that was now one of Britain's most important allies.[27] The series was completed in 1995 in seventy-five volumes: United States participation in the project ended in 1979 but the British editors, led by Ronald Wheatley from 1960 until his death in 1985, continued to meet their German and French counterparts for some years to come.[28] And until the beginning of the twenty-first century, the German section retained a presence in the Foreign Office in the person of one editorial assistant who

[25] My former colleague Keith Hamilton (in an email of 16 April 2021) offers a valuable corrective to this view: 'Might I just say a word in defence of the much-maligned editors of *Die Grosse Politik*? They were certainly not alone amongst editors and historians in adopting a distinctly patriotic stance in the aftermath of the Great War. Headlam-Morley, who was responsible for volume XI of *British Documents on the Origins of the War* (BD), never quite freed himself from his role as a wartime propagandist. Moreover, Gooch and Temperley could sometimes be very economical with the documents they published. The section in volume I of the series dealing with The Hague peace conference of 1899 includes no more than the final paragraph of a twenty-seven-page War Office memorandum, arguing against any limitation of armaments. Britain's representatives at The Hague were able to rely on the Germans to make their case for them, and the editorial note at the beginning of the BD conference section reads: "The various questions discussed at the Conference … are discussed at full length in *GP*, XV, 197–346" (see BD, I, p. 223) – a wonderful opt out. In this instance British diplomacy and its editors owed much to those villains of the Wilhelmstrasse.'

[26] Quoted in D. Cameron Watt, 'British historians, the war guilt issue, and post-war Germanophobia: A documentary note', *Historical Journal*, xxxvi (1993), 179–85 (p. 181).

[27] Ibid., p. 179.

[28] Like the current series, *Akten zur Auswärtigen Politik der Bundesrepublik Deutschland* (AAPD), DGFP was produced under the auspices of the Institut für Zeitgeschichte, Munich, in collaboration with the German Foreign Office: see <https://www.ifz-muenchen. de/aktuelles/themen/akten-zur-auswaertigen-politik>. The entire series has been digitized by the Bayrische Staatsbibliothek: <https://digi20.digitale-sammlungen.de/de/fs1/start/ static.html>. For an account of British participation in the last years of the project see Eleanor Breuning, 'International cooperation', in FCO Historians, *Papers Presented at the Seminar for Editors of Diplomatic Documents, Held in the Foreign and Commonwealth Office on 9 November 1989* (Occasional Papers No. 2, London, 1989), pp. 39–43.

had been there since the 1950s, along with a few surviving files of long-forgotten queries.

The peacetime official histories

By the mid-1960s all of the civil series of the Second World War official histories had been published, along with the bulk of the military series, and the future of the Cabinet Office Historical Section was in doubt. It was rescued, and the official history programme given a new lease of life, by the then Prime Minister, Harold Wilson. As leader of the opposition, Wilson had been interested in arguments that the fifty-year limit established by the 1958 Public Records Act should be reduced to forty or even thirty years. In a memorandum of July 1965, less than a year after assuming the premiership, Wilson came down strongly in favour of a thirty-year rule and added two further recommendations: first, that the range of official histories should be extended 'to include selected periods or episodes of peace-time history' under a new system of management by a bi-partisan committee of Privy Counsellors; second, that, either alternatively or in addition, selected documents on peacetime history from other government departments might be published 'on the same lines as the Foreign Office series of documents on British Foreign Policy'.[29]

In 1966 the Head of the Historical Section, W.I. McIndoe, confided to Rohan Butler that the introduction of a new peacetime series, in addition to a thirty-year rule, might have been an oversight, since the proposal 'had originated as a sop to historians at a time when it was still contemplated that the closed period for public records might be longer than thirty years'.[30] But Wilson must have known what he was doing, and it is likely that he was influenced by the enormous success of a civil history published in 1964 that did not originate in the Cabinet Office, Margaret Gowing's *Britain and Atomic Energy, 1939–1945*. Drawing on her years of experience of working with Keith Hancock and sponsored by an enlightened employer, the United Kingdom Atomic Energy Authority, Gowing's book caught the spirit of the times and became a model to be emulated as the new programme of peacetime histories took shape.[31]

[29] Memorandum of 27 July 1965, printed in Keith Wilson, *Forging the Collective Memory: Government and International Historians through Two World Wars* (Providence, RI, and Oxford, 1996), pp. 289–93.

[30] Butler minute, 'Official histories and the proposed thirty-year rule', 26 May 1966, The National Archives (TNA), FO 370/2906.

[31] Followed by her own peacetime history, co-authored with Lorna Arnold, *Independence and Deterrence: Britain and Atomic Energy, 1945–52* (2 vols, London, 1974).

Following agreement with the leaders of the Liberal and Conservative opposition, Wilson's proposals became law in August 1966. Rohan Butler, who had been appointed historical adviser to the Foreign Secretary by Lord Home in 1962, remained wary of any encroachment on the Foreign Office's traditional freedom to publish documents on British foreign policy, or any suggestion that the new narrative histories might include episodes of post-war diplomatic history. Although he accepted 'the possibility of a confidential study of British attempts to enter the Common Market', the Suez crisis was another matter: Butler felt that the proposed committee of Privy Counsellors 'would be likely to encourage much invidious log-rolling for particular projects (e.g. Suez) among historians, who would doubtless know who were the Privy Counsellors in question'. On the other hand, Butler accepted that other 'external' departments should be allowed to publish documents, and he welcomed the proposal of the Commonwealth Relations Office (which would merge with the Colonial Office in 1966 to form the Commonwealth Office) 'to sponsor a documentary publication of the last phase of British rule in India, in deliberate preference to a narrative history'.[32] This was to prove one of the most successful of the post-war official history projects. Launched in 1967 with Nicholas Mansergh as editor-in-chief, *The Transfer of Power, 1942–7* was completed in twelve magisterial volumes between 1970 and 1983.[33]

Official history had not yet finished with the war. In response to the growing body of unofficial history and memoirs (some highly contentious) devoted to special operations and European resistance in the Second World War, M.R.D. Foot's *SOE in France* was published in 1966.[34] Following F.W. Winterbotham's revelations in *The Ultra Secret* (1974), Sir Harry Hinsley's *British Intelligence in the Second World War* appeared in five volumes between 1979 and 1990. The publication of the fifth volume, *Strategic Deception*, by Sir Michael Howard, had been prevented on security grounds by the then Prime Minister, Margaret Thatcher, and appeared only after she had left office.[35] The 1980s saw other missteps. Two further SOE histories were published by Oxford University Press, but the second of these, Charles Cruickshank's *SOE in Scandinavia* (1986), incurred scathing judgements on

[32] Butler minute, 26 May 1966 (note 30 above).

[33] It is worth mentioning in this connection the important *British Documents on the End of Empire* (BDEEP) series available at <https://bdeep.org>.

[34] Christopher J. Murphy, 'The origins of *SOE in France*', *Historical Journal*, xlvi (2003), 935–52.

[35] Charles Moore, *Margaret Thatcher: The Authorized Biography*, vol. 2, *Everything She Wants* (London, 2015), p. 137.

its inaccuracies as well as on 'the privatization of official history'.[36] It may have been for this reason that the SOE sub-series was halted for some years and that, when it was resumed, the task of writing *SOE in the Low Countries* (2001) was entrusted to the safe hands of M.R.D Foot, followed by the two volumes of Sir Brooks Richards's *Secret Flotillas* (2004).

The first round of peacetime histories got off to a strong start. Beginning in 1975 with Sir Norman Chester's *Nationalisation of British Industry*, it included a four-volume history of *Environmental Planning, 1939–69* by J.B. Cullingworth and G. E. Cherry (1975–81), D.J. Morgan's five-volume *History of Colonial Development* (1980) and the first volume of L.S Pressnell's magisterial *External Economic Policy since the War* (1986).[37] But if the 1950s and 1960s had been the golden age of wartime official history, the first two decades of the twenty-first century saw a second round of peacetime histories reach a new peak in terms of both output and quality.[38] Publication had now passed from Her Majesty's Stationery Office, via a brief interlude with Frank Cass, to Taylor & Francis under the Routledge imprint; and the contract (from 1999) was with a new body, the Whitehall History Publishing Group, comprising the Cabinet Office, the Foreign and Commonwealth Office and the Ministry of Defence. The purpose of the programme was defined in 2005, by what had now become the Histories, Openness and Records Unit of the Cabinet Office, as being 'to provide authoritative histories in their own right; a reliable secondary source for historians until all the records are available in The National Archives; and

[36] Olav Riste, 'Open season for rewriting history', *The Times*, 10 June 1986, p. 12. The other volume, Charles Cruickshank's *SOE in the Far East* (1983), did not attract the same level of criticism.

[37] There seems to be no publicly available complete list of the Cabinet Office peacetime histories, but see Appendix III for my attempt to provide one.

[38] Accurate information on the recent history of the Cabinet Office official histories programme is remarkably difficult to find. The Cabinet Office's website (<https://www.gov.uk/government/organisations/cabinet-office>) makes no mention of official history at all. The best starting point is a research briefing, produced in support of a House of Lords short debate on the programme in December 2015: <https://lordslibrary.parliament.uk/research-briefings/lif-2015-0056>. This leads to a longer report by Nicola Newson, which can be downloaded. This report in turn contains a number of valuable links, including one (the only one I have been able to find) to Sir Joe Pilling's important 2009 report on the official histories programme, <https://assets.publishing.service.gov.uk/government/uploads/system/uploads/attachment_data/file/62233/future-plans-government.pdf>. Perhaps the clearest description of how the system is supposed to work is contained in an archived article by the late Rodney Lowe (official historian of the Civil Service), 'Official history', <https://archives.history.ac.uk/makinghistory/resources/articles/official_history.html>.

a "fund of experience" for future government use'.[39] The Unit went on to describe how topics were chosen and commissioned:

> The topics for inclusion in the official history programme are selected initially by the Official Cabinet Committee on Official Histories (OH) on which all major government departments are represented. The topics are then considered by a Group of Privy Counsellors, one from each major political party, currently comprising Lord [Denis] Healey, Lord [Geoffrey] Howe, and Lord [Bill] Rodgers of Quarry Bank. The Privy Counsellors' approval provides the necessary authority for the historian to have access to records of all previous administrations.
>
> Historians of eminence in their field are identified, after consultation with appropriate government departments, and are appointed by the Prime Minister. They are then given access to all relevant material in government archives, whether publicly available or not. The official historian writes the history from his/her own perspective on the basis of the full information. Any security issues connected with the historians' use of still sensitive material are then addressed before the manuscript goes to the publisher.

What this meant in practice was indicated by the importance and interest of the subjects selected in 2000, when the OH committee and the group of Privy Counsellors last met, as well as the calibre of the historians the programme was able to attract: to give only a few examples, Sir Lawrence Freedman's *The Falklands Campaign* (2005); Terry Gourvish's *The Channel Tunnel* (2006); and Alan Milward's history of Britain and European integration, *The Rise and Fall of a National Strategy 1945–1963* (2002).[40]

Beneath the surface, however, all was not well. In part this had to do with the impact of the austerity policies introduced after the economic crisis of 2008; but there were already signs of a slackening of official interest and support. It was significant, for instance, that when government departments responded to the Cabinet Secretary's request for proposals for a new round of official histories, in October 2007, their suggestions were not followed up: the OH committee never met and the Privy Counsellors were never consulted.[41] Clearly sensing something amiss, Lord Rodgers, the most active of the three Privy Counsellors, initiated the first of three House of

[39] Typically, this is not a web page in current use, but one archived by The National Archives: <https://webarchive.nationalarchives.gov.uk/20080205143007/http://www.cabinetoffice.gov.uk/publicationscheme/published_information/1/officialhistory.aspx>. The 'fund of experience' was a phrase dating back to the wartime Cabinet Secretary, Sir Edward Bridges, expressing an optimism that had largely been belied in practice: see Hancock, *Country and Calling*, pp. 196–7.
[40] See Appendix III and comment in note 37 above.
[41] This is based on my own recollections and notes I made at the time.

Lords debates on the future of the programme in February 2008, with two others following in July 2013 and December 2015 (by which time both of his fellow Counsellors had died).[42] All three debates elicited much support for official history on the part of Lord Rodgers's fellow peers, including historians such as Lord Hennessy, Lord Bew and Lord Lexden. Moreover, Lord Rodgers's first intervention had a positive outcome: the appointment in December 2008 of Sir Joe Pilling, a former Permanent Secretary of the Northern Ireland Department, to conduct an investigation into the official histories programme. Sir Joe produced his report in April 2009, with a supplementary report on the publishing side by Bill Hamilton, a well-known literary agent.[43]

The Pilling report came down strongly in favour of maintaining the official history programme:

> It seems to be greatly to our credit as a country, to politicians of succeeding generations and all parties and to public servants of all descriptions that we have had a sustained programme of histories written by distinguished, independent people free to reach their own judgments after full access to papers and people. I have come to see it as the gold standard of accountability to the country from those who have been privileged to hold senior office.

Sir Joe also recommended that it should continue to be managed by the Cabinet Office. He suggested, however, that the programme's aims should be made more explicit; that its links with the academic world should be strengthened by the addition of an advisory council; that its name should be changed to the Public History Programme in order to enable it to reach a wider public; and that official historians should be encouraged to raise the profile of their research by publishing articles and delivering conference papers. Bill Hamilton, meanwhile, had some sharp comments about the high costs and low profile of the official history series, and the difficulty of persuading commercial publishers to take an interest in either the series as a whole or individual volumes:

> The Programme has a low profile except in Whitehall and among some historians. None of the publishers or literary editors that I talked to – and few historians – were conscious of the series or what it consisted of. There is plainly a lot of work to do before the histories get the public recognition they deserve, or before the historians and Cabinet Office get a return on their investment

---

[42] *House of Lords Hansard*, vol. 698, 5 February 2008, cols 1013–25; vol. 747, 10 July 2013, cols 335–51; vol. 767, cols 189–200.
[43] <https://assets.publishing.service.gov.uk/government/uploads/system/uploads/attachment_data/file/62233/future-plans-government.pdf>.

of time and money. Whether or not individual volumes are intended to be accessible to a popular audience, they represent high level history written by high quality historians from privileged sources, and give a rare insight into aspects of government. Currently there is very little public recognition of these unique qualities.

By November 2009 the Cabinet Office had come up with draft responses to the report's recommendations, and government departments had been asked for their views.[44] There is no sign that these responses were ever acted upon. The next we hear is a letter of August 2010 in which the Cabinet Secretary, Sir Gus O'Donnell, told the three Privy Counsellors: 'Given the current challenging economic climate, I am sure that there is likely to be a hiatus in commissioning titles.'[45] 'That is how it was,' Lord Rodgers told his fellow peers five years later, in December 2015; 'There was no further explanation and nothing further about how to implement the Pilling report.' Six years beyond that debate, the hiatus continues and there is still no clarity about the fate of the Cabinet Office's official histories programme. The most recent volumes in the series have maintained its reputation for high quality but, for the moment, they are likely to be the last.[46]

The Cabinet Office histories faced other challenges. Their expensive and poorly marketed volumes had to compete with the popular and reasonably priced 'authorized' histories commissioned by the intelligence agencies –

---

[44] Personal recollection.

[45] Quoted by Lord Rodgers in the Lords debate of 10 December 2015, col. 190.

[46] For example, Matthew Jones, *The Official History of the UK Strategic Nuclear Deterrent* (2 vols, 2017); Stephen Wall, *The Official History of Britain and the European Community*, vol. 3 (2018). At a late stage in production, the Cabinet Office transferred these two works to the Ministry of Defence and the FCO respectively to oversee their completion. On 9 July 2019 Lord Rodgers asked a further three questions about the Cabinet Office official history programme and the FCO's documentary series. In response to his question 'whether Whitehall History Publishing still exists; if so, (1) what is its role, and (2) how is it managed and by whom; and if not, who is responsible for the publication of material it previously produced', Lord Young of Cookham replied: 'The Whitehall History Publishing, comprised of several historical branches of government departments and led by the Cabinet Office, produces material on historical matters and themes to meet individual departmental requirements. The next publication is due out in autumn 2019.' In response to Lord Rodgers's question when HMG 'last reviewed the possible resumption of producing official histories', Lord Young replied: 'The Government's official history series is intended to provide authoritative histories in their own right. Two volumes of Criminal Justice history were published earlier this year. The next publication is due out in autumn 2019.' This did not, of course, address the question of whether any further official histories were in the pipeline. <https://members.parliament.uk/member/940/writtenquestions#expand-1137959>.

first Christopher Andrew's history of MI5, *Defence of the Realm* (2009), then Keith Jeffery's *MI6* (2010) and, most recently, John Ferris's *Behind the Enigma: The Authorised History of GCHQ* (2020).[47] Official historians also had to compete with the claims of academic historians to provide historical lessons as relevant to current problems as anything they could offer, and in forms much more readily accessible. History and Policy, founded in 2002, has produced more than 200 policy papers and has established strong links with departments such as the Treasury, the Home Office, the Department of Transport and the Cabinet Office itself, as have the Mile End Institute at Queen Mary University of London, and the Strand Group at King's College London.[48] However, while they have done much to raise historical awareness across government, it is difficult to quantify their direct influence on decision making.[49] Theoretically, it must be easier for busy officials and ministers to read short policy papers online than heavy works of official history, but it remains unclear whether they do so.

Documents on British Foreign Policy Overseas

The malaise afflicting the Cabinet Office programme had wider causes. The privileged access to closed official files enjoyed by official historians had already been compromised by the thirty-year rule. The Freedom of Information Act of 2000, which came into effect on 1 January 2005, followed by the introduction of a new twenty-year rule in 2013, undermined any claim to exclusivity still further. These changes also affected the work of the Foreign Office historians, who had been engaged since the 1980s in a publishing project designed to record the history of British foreign policy since 1945, just as DBFP had done for the inter-war period. The idea of producing a successor to DBFP dated back to the mid-1960s, when completion of the inter-war series was in sight. In 1966 Rohan Butler reported that he was conducting a pilot survey and had already identified three potential problems: first, 'the formidable increase in the bulk of the archives'; second, 'special and possibly delicate considerations arising from the Cold War'; and, third, 'ditto in respect of decolonization and its impact

---

[47] All published by Bloomsbury, and all with contracts negotiated by Bill Hamilton on terms very favourable to the agencies concerned.

[48] <http://www.historyandpolicy.org>; <https://www.qmul.ac.uk/mei/about-us>; <https://thestrandgroup.kcl.ac.uk>.

[49] For a helpful discussion see Matthew Grant, 'History and policy', in *A Practical Guide to Studying History: Skills and Approaches*, ed. Tracey Loughran (London, 2017), pp. 233–47.

on British foreign policy'.[50] His proposed solution to the first problem was to produce smaller, more selective volumes than had been the practice with DBFP, but to supplement these with what he called 'calendars': lists that referred to a much larger body of unpublished documents which would be microfilmed and made publicly available:

> Thus the publication of each volume of documents and calendars might inaugurate a joint venture between the editors and serious students among their readers. The Foreign Office would secure the benefit of authoritative documentary publication plus the additional benefit, one would hope, of original research by independent historians in support of the published material, and also of their increased goodwill.

This was the solution adopted for the new series, *Documents on British Policy Overseas* (DBPO), which was announced by the Foreign Secretary, Sir Alec Douglas-Home, in Parliament on 2 July 1973.[51] It was nearly a decade since Butler had started his pilot survey, and it would be a further eleven years before the first volume appeared. The delay was a setback from which DBPO has never fully recovered. Nor did the first volume in series I (1945–50), *The Conference at Potsdam, July–August 1945* (1984), weighing in at nearly 1300 pages, meet Butler's original criterion, despite its use of calendars and microfiches. Published two years after Butler's retirement and eight years after the post-1945 documents had begun to be released by the Public Record Office (PRO) under the thirty-year rule, it threatened rather to fulfil his prophecy 'that if we are not careful any new documentary publication will run the danger of strangling itself with the editors progressing slower and slower in producing more and more volumes which fewer and fewer people can find time to read'.[52] The first volume of series II (1950–5), covering the early years of European integration, was nearly as large.[53]

The editorial team, now led by Margaret Pelly and Roger Bullen of LSE, reverted to Butler's original idea of producing smaller volumes and achieved a respectable output over the next decade without, however, catching up with the documents released annually by the PRO. By now, DBPO was

[50] Memorandum of 18 October 1966, 'Historical presentation of recent British foreign policy', TNA, FO 370/2906.

[51] For details of internal FCO discussions, including the question of how to handle sensitive material, see FCO Historians, *History at the Heart of Diplomacy*, pp. 50–2, <https://issuu.com/fcohistorians/docs/history_at_the_heart_of_diplomacy-w>.

[52] Butler memorandum of 18 October 1966, TNA, FO 370/2906.

[53] *The Schuman Plan, the Council of Europe and Western European Integration 1950–1952*, ed. Roger Bullen and M.E. Pelly (1986).

achieving a solid reputation among the academic community: Zara Steiner chose one of its volumes as her book of the year in the *Financial Times*, noting that it was a 'superbly edited publication which amateur strategists will find more gripping than most studies of the British contribution to the cold war'.[54] This was a period in which the FCO historians became more outward-looking, organizing (in 1987) their first seminar for external academics and (in 1989) the first International Conference of Editors of Diplomatic Documents (ICEDD), beginning what was to become a biennial series.[55] But it was also a period marked by tragedy – the premature death of Roger Bullen in 1988, barely a year after his appointment as historical adviser to the Secretary of State, Sir Geoffrey Howe – and the end of the era of part-time external editors that had begun with Gooch and Temperley. DBPO now became a wholly in-house operation, led by Margaret Pelly, along with two former editorial assistants with DBFP, Heather Yasamee and Gill Bennett. On Pelly's retirement in 1990, she was succeeded as head of Historical Branch by Yasamee, and as editor by Keith Hamilton from University College of Wales, Aberystwyth, the first external academic to be recruited as a full-time editor directly employed by the FCO.

The early 1990s were a period of increasingly open government: in 1992 the existence of the intelligence agencies was publicly avowed for the first time;[56] Foreign Secretary Douglas Hurd announced a re-review of all closed FCO records (leading, among other things, to the release of documents relating to Rudolf Hess and the return of the Krupp papers to Germany); and William Waldegrave launched an initiative inviting historians to propose blocks of papers that might be considered for release. At the same time, it was becoming evident that the timetable for publication of DBPO was falling further and further behind the PRO's annual release programme. What was the point, some people at the FCO argued, in publishing records that were already publicly available at the PRO? It was in this atmosphere that the editors of DBPO took the decision to launch a new third series which would publish documents less than thirty years old: in other words, ones that had not been released to the Public Record Office and that no one

[54] Quoted in FCO Historians, *History at the Heart of Diplomacy*, pp. 106–8. Her choice was series II, vol. II, *The London Conferences: Anglo-American Relations and Cold War Strategy January–June 1950* (1987).

[55] The papers given to the 1987 seminar are published at <https://issuu.com/fcohistorians/docs/hpop_1>; the proceedings of the 1989 conference are published in 'International cooperation', in FCO Historians, *Papers Presented at the Seminar for Editors of Diplomatic Documents*. For the ICEDD see <https://diplomatic-documents.org>.

[56] Strictly speaking, the existence of MI5 was avowed in 1989 with the Security Service Act, that of SIS and GCHQ in 1994 with the Intelligence Services Act. 1992 was the year in which the chiefs of the two main agencies were allowed to be named publicly.

else had yet had the opportunity to see. There would be no more calendars and no more microfiches. The new policy, which tacitly recognized that series I and II might never be completed, owed much to Keith Hamilton's research in FCO files from the 1970s, in preparation for his in-house history of the Know How Fund,[57] which had convinced him that there was scope for a DBPO volume on the Helsinki Conference of 1975. It was carried forward by Gill Bennett, who had left the editorial team in 1991, but returned to the new position of Chief Historian in 1995. Her first volume in series III, *Britain and the Soviet Union 1968–1972* (1997), exemplified the new approach, using the documents, interspersed with plenty of editorial comment, to tell a compelling and often dramatic story. The second volume, *The Conference on Security and Cooperation in Europe 1972–1975*, edited by Hamilton, was published at the same time. Like its successor, *Détente in Europe 1972–1976* (2001), it was more traditional in approach, but both broke new ground in documenting the history of European détente in the 1970s.

After the turn of the century, however, the inexorable operation of the thirty-year rule, combined with the diversion of the editorial team to other tasks (itself a measure of their growing esteem within the FCO)[58] and the emergence of new technologies which seemed to threaten the viability of traditional print volumes, led to a further reassessment. In 2002 it was decided that in future DBPO would take the form of hybrid volumes, with introduction and critical apparatus in hard copy, accompanied by a CD-ROM containing facsimiles of the original documents. Ultimately only two volumes appeared in this format. *The Year of Europe: America, Europe and the Energy Crisis 1972–1974* (2006) contained 568 documents on CD-ROM: almost as many as in the first volumes of the series, and in a far more compact form. But by the time *Berlin in the Cold War 1948–1990* appeared in 2009, containing 509 documents (now on DVD), technology had moved on. The format had never proved attractive to readers and the ubiquity of the internet had made it as redundant as the microfiche.

---

[57] A much-revised and expanded version was later published as *Transformational Diplomacy after the Cold War: Britain's Know How Fund in Post-Communist Europe, 1989–2003* (London and New York, 2013).

[58] In 1996 the historians were commissioned by Foreign Secretary Malcolm Rifkind to investigate the British archives for information on the Nazi theft of gold and other Jewish property: their reports are available at <https://issuu.com/fcohistorians/docs/history_notes_cover_hphn_11> and <https://issuu.com/fcohistorians/docs/history_notes_cover_hphn_12>. In 1998 Gill Bennett was commissioned by Foreign Secretary Robin Cook to write a report on the origins of the Zinoviev Letter of 1924, a source of long-standing grievance on the part of the Labour Party. For the full story see Gill Bennett, *The Zinoviev Letter: The Conspiracy that Never Dies* (Oxford, 2018).

One of my first decisions after succeeding Gill Bennett as Chief Historian in 2005 was to revert to hard copy. Since then, production of DBPO has averaged roughly one volume a year, still published by Routledge. Most have been drawn from what was once, but is no longer, the 'closed' period – in practice this has largely meant the Thatcher era – but we have also produced three further volumes in series I, covering such vital topics as the Marshall Plan and the North Atlantic Treaty, meaning that coverage of the early Cold War is now largely complete. On the other hand, there are still no volumes at all for the period between 1952 and 1968. Since 2008 the printed volumes have been augmented by a digital version, published by ProQuest, which includes all three series produced since 1924 – *British Documents on the Origins of the War, Documents on British Foreign Policy* and *Documents on British Policy Overseas* – and has all the advantages of instant searchability.[59] The snag, as always, is cost. The price of hardback volumes averages £100 each, although this is alleviated by cheaper paperback editions and e-books; the cost of subscriptions to ProQuest can be borne only by large institutional libraries. This contrasts with such freely available and easily searchable series as *Foreign Relations of the United States* and *Diplomatic Documents of Switzerland.*[60]

Yet we continue to insist – rightly, in my view – that the practice of selecting and publishing diplomatic documents remains a valuable activity: one not rendered redundant even when the relevant archives are fully open to inspection, or when parts of their contents are randomly revealed to individual researchers by the Freedom of Information Act. It is not just a matter of providing a convenient insight into the documents held by the National Archives for those who live a long way from London, or a useful teaching tool for lecturers in international history, although DBPO does perform both of these functions. There is still a place for a coherently organized body of documents grouped around a clearly identified topic, and placed in context by a full scholarly apparatus. Not that DBPO would ever claim to have the last word on any subject: indeed, its editors can recall their own delight as young researchers when they found something in the archives that earlier editors of DBFP had missed – but something, on the other hand, they might never have discovered if DBFP had not provided the clue.

Moreover, I think we can claim that in many respects DBPO is better than DBFP – better, certainly, than the early volumes. There is, after all, a certain perfunctoriness in the brevity of Woodward's and Butler's prefaces

59 <https://about.proquest.com/products-services/dbpo.html>.
60 <https://history.state.gov/historicaldocuments; https://www.dodis.ch/en/home>.

and their willingness to skim the surface level of telegrams and despatches without delving deeper. Taylor and Butterfield were right to lament the lack of internal minutes and the absence of documents reflecting any perspectives other than those of the Foreign Office. DBPO reveals the FCO's internal policy debates as well as its interactions with other parts of the government apparatus – above all, No. 10 Downing Street. If Margaret Thatcher's indignant marginal comments and vigorous underlinings are indispensable to an understanding of British foreign policy in the 1980s, what are we to make of an account of Munich that tells us nothing directly about the views of Neville Chamberlain?[61] We trawl more widely than our predecessors in other respects. As early as 1997, Gill Bennett's volume on Britain and the Soviet Union printed a 1972 'Report by the Joint Intelligence Committee on the Soviet Threat', and most of our subsequent volumes have contained some intelligence material, often from the files of the FCO's Permanent Under-Secretary's Department (PUSD), which handled liaison with the intelligence agencies. An illustration of how the intelligence dimension can transform our understanding of earlier periods of British foreign policy is provided by a recent publication on the Potsdam Conference of 1945 which combines a selection of documents from the first eight volumes of DBPO, series I, with a number of newly released documents relating to the Soviet defector Igor Gouzenko (codename 'Corby').[62] The juxtaposition shows how Western governments engaged in the task of making the post-war world were unsettled by this first glimpse into a Soviet espionage network whose full extent was yet to be revealed.

Does official history have a future? There may be signs of a revival of interest at the Cabinet Office. The Cabinet Secretary appointed in September 2020, Simon Case, is a former student of Peter Hennessy, a powerful advocate of official history; some senior ministers are also said to be historically minded. It is also reassuring that Professor John Bew has been appointed the Prime Minister's chief foreign policy adviser. Might government departments choose to commission their own histories, as the Ministry of Defence has recently done with its authorized history of British defence economic

---

[61] It may be appropriate here to pay tribute to the remarkable collection of original documents made available on the website of the Margaret Thatcher Foundation: <https://www.margaretthatcher.org>.

[62] *Britain and the Making of the Post-War World: The Potsdam Conference and Beyond*, ed. Gill Bennett and Richard Smith (2020), <https://issuu.com/fcohistorians/docs/britain_and_the_making_of_the_post-war_world_with_>; also available at <https://www.amazon.co.uk/Britain-making-Post-War-World-Conference/dp/B08CWCGSNR>.

intelligence?[63] Each of the armed services, after all, retains its own historical branch with its own publishing tradition quite separate from that of the Cabinet Office. Could there be official histories of recent conflicts such as the first Gulf War or Afghanistan, or has the work of official history been superseded by that of official inquiries? After Chilcot, will we ever want an official history of the Iraq War? Will there be an official inquiry into the government's handling of Brexit, or might the work be assigned to an official historian? Or perhaps official history in the form of books has no future at all, and government should instead have one or more 'chief historians' or 'chief historical advisers', as was suggested some years ago by Sir David Cannadine and more recently by Sir Anthony Seldon.[64]

As for the publication of diplomatic documents, this may be an activity whose heyday was in the 1920s or the 1950s; but it is one in which both governments and academic institutions across the world still find it worthwhile to invest. The website of the ICEDD lists seventeen countries that publish series of diplomatic documents: they include some where the practice has lapsed, such as the Netherlands; others where it has lapsed and then been revived, as in Italy; and others of relatively recent origin which have already made substantial progress.[65] *Documents on Irish Policy*, launched in 1997, has published twelve volumes covering the period from 1919 to 1965.[66] *Polish Diplomatic Documents*, established as recently as 2005, has been even more productive, having published twenty-seven volumes covering both the period of the Second Republic (1918–45) and that of the communist era (1945–89).[67] At their biennial conferences, the editors still debate methodology. Some questions, such as whether volumes should be organized chronologically or by theme, date back to the beginnings of their craft in the 1920s.[68] Others are more fundamental. Will it be possible

[63] Peter Davies, *British Defence Economic Intelligence: A Cold War in Whitehall 1929–90* (London, 2019).

[64] Sir David Cannadine spoke at a History and Policy meeting at the Cabinet War Rooms, London, on 5 December 2007; Anthony Seldon, 'Why every government department needs a resident historian', *Prospect*, 1 May 2020, <https://www.prospectmagazine.co.uk/politics/government-department-chief-historian-whitehall-number-10-coronavirus-covid-brexit>.

[65] <https://diplomatic-documents.org/editions>.

[66] <www.difp.ie>.

[67] <https://diplomatic-documents.org/information/?pdb=27>. Two volumes, covering the periods 1918–19 and 1938–9, have been published in English translation.

[68] In the bibliography of A.J.P. Taylor, *The Struggle for Mastery in Europe 1848–1918* (Oxford, 1954), pp. 578–81, can be found typically trenchant comments on the pros and cons of chronology versus topic. By arranging their documents by subject, Taylor wrote, the editors of the *Grosse Politik* concealed 'the connexion of one topic with another'. Gooch and Temperley then seemed to have adopted the German model 'without reflection' and 'described it as "the British way" – a phrase often used in this country to cloak any irrational

to edit and publish documents at all when paper archives no longer exist: when communications are entirely digital and governments have largely abandoned record-keeping as traditionally understood? Or, conversely, will it be possible to place a larger volume of records in the public sphere than ever before? Here the Turkish Foreign Ministry may hold the key to the future, having completed a project to digitize Turkey's entire diplomatic record from the foundation of the Turkish Republic in 1919 to 2001, employing hundreds of staff working in purpose-built facilities.[69] And here, perhaps, we may come close to Butterfield's ideal of 'a world of independent historians, choosing their own subjects for research, and allowed by the government free access to the archives'.[70]

---

act'. Only the French got it right: 'The documents are arranged in chronological order, while a table at the beginning of each volume sorts them into subjects. It is difficult to understand how any subsequent editor can have strayed from this arrangement.' The *Grosse Politik* remains the model followed by the British editors, although the current German series, AAPD, has adopted the chronological approach. The Italians, however, have supplemented their original chronological series, *I Documenti Diplomatici Italiani*, with a new thematic series, *Documenti sulla Politica Internazionale dell'Italia*: see <https://diplomatic-documents. org/information/?pdb=24>.

[69] As reported to the ICEDD conference in Washington in 2015, sixty-five million pages were planned to be digitized within three years by a 300-strong skilled work force operating in two shifts. They had hoped to achieve an output of 100,000 pages a day but were actually achieving 130,000. For an excellent explanatory video, see <http://diad.mfa.gov.tr/short-about-the-archives.en.mfa>.

[70] Butterfield to Blaxall, 9 May 1952 (Appendix I below).

4. Why bother with Butterfield?

We seem to have come a long way from Butterfield, yet the story of the making of official history in the United Kingdom over the last seventy years reveals a recurrent tension between the demands of government and those of academic historians that he would have found very familiar. And between government and academics, of course, are the official historians. Are there any lessons to be drawn by official historians today from Butterfield's encounter with their predecessors seventy years ago? Much of what Woodward and Medlicott wrote in response to Butterfield is instantly familiar. Like Woodward, we complain that no one in the Foreign Office seems interested in our work; that busy officials never have the time to read the drafts we send them. Like Medlicott, we have the run of the archives and we smile knowingly when academics claim that 'MI5' must have gone through thousands of files 'with a fine-tooth comb' before they were released to a gullible public.[1] And we agree with Woodward that there always exists a check on our honesty in the fact that the archives from which we make our selection will one day – perhaps very soon – be fully open. Like Woodward, we 'don't want to get the posthumous reputation of a faker of history'.[2]

Yet we also know that some of Butterfield's criticisms are uncomfortably close to home. We do not knowingly practise self-censorship, but there are many documents we do not even try to include in our selection because we know they will not pass the scrutiny of the sensitivity reviewer: items to do with secret intelligence or the Royal Family, for instance. And if Gooch and Temperley or Woodward and Butler were not wholly independent because they drew a government salary and were subject to the Official Secrets Act, how independent are we as full-time civil servants?[3] Perhaps the reason why we are allowed to go about our business with little interference is simply because our work is less politically sensitive, less vital to the nation's self-image, than that of our predecessors who documented the origins of two world wars.

---

[1] A claim made at the time of the discovery of the FCO's colonial or 'migrated' archive in 2011.

[2] Woodward to Butterfield, 28 July 1949, BUTT/130/4.

[3] In fact Gooch, who had a substantial private income, chose to work without payment. Temperley, having originally proposed £500 a year, a figure thought too low by the Foreign Office librarian, was paid £750: Frank Eyck, *G.P. Gooch: A Study in History and Politics* (London and Basingstoke, 1982), pp. 340–1. I do not know how much the editors of DBFP or the early editors of DBPO were paid.

On the other hand, being 'embedded' within government departments confers a level of understanding about process, and of the relative importance of issues and parts of the governmental system, which is impossible for complete outsiders to achieve. If there are documents we cannot publish, we try hard to find others that make the same point without the same complications. Being civil servants, in the sense of being employed in the system, helps us know how to do this. Only official historians with clearance have privileged access to the full archive, even though that does not confer an automatic right to publish. But the number of times permission has been refused, over a long period, is very small.[4] And in current circumstances, external scrutiny by critical academics and organizations pushes both the archives and historians to be as transparent as possible. Making sense of the material would be difficult without the help of 'insiders' like us. Being a civil servant, or at least subject to civil service rules for a while, is the trade-off for access, knowledge and understanding that our non-official colleagues, however critical they are, are generally grateful for.

As to the first of Butterfield's two central maxims, we can agree that no government wants the public to know all the truth; the problem is to work out exactly what this means in practice: not least because, if the deception has been successful, we simply don't know what has been concealed or destroyed. The cases we know about are the ones where the attempt has failed, as with the Windsor papers or, to take a more recent example, the so-called 'migrated archive' of colonial government records that was revealed in 2011 as a result of litigation against the Foreign and Commonwealth Office over the treatment of Mau Mau suspects in Kenya in the 1950s.[5] Here the concealment was real, but with a variety of motives, including the desire to protect those who had collaborated with colonial regimes from retribution by post-colonial governments. And if the British government had been really determined to cover its tracks it would have simply have ordered the documents to be destroyed. Except in very few cases, that did not happen. The problem was not so much the one identified by Butterfield – that the present generation of official historians and archivists might be honest but later generations less so – but that later generations simply forgot

---

[4] For examples from the early volumes of DBPO, see Margaret Pelly, 'Sensitive documents and editorial freedom', in FCO Historians, *Papers Presented at the Seminar for Editors of Diplomatic Documents*, pp. 44–7.

[5] Shohei Sato, '"Operation Legacy": Britain's destruction and concealment of colonial records worldwide', *Journal of Imperial and Commonwealth History*, xlv (2017), 697–719. However, a large part of that archive is low-grade administrative material that no one thought would be of any value, including TNA, who originally refused to take it and advised the FCO to destroy it on more than one occasion.

or never knew about the original concealment, so that they could walk past the documents on the shelves every day without understanding their significance. The key problem is therefore not the mythical secret drawer, but the loss of institutional memory: one that will only get worse as the decline of official record-keeping accelerates.

Of course the preoccupation with the secret drawer, or some version of it, is not confined to Butterfield. It is at the heart of all criticism of official history: outsiders distrust it because they don't know everything about how it works. One of the most common fallacies pursued by critics, not just of official history but of archival processes in general, is the assumption that if something is withheld or kept secret it must be important. This is not necessarily true, particularly in regard to intelligence-related material, which is always only one piece of the jigsaw and is rarely decisive. The same applies to Foreign Office minutes. Although we can all agree that minutes and other annotations can be significant and, if so, should be included, they can also be misleading. It is precisely the ordered, hierarchical character of Foreign Office documents, especially those of the inter-war period, that can tempt the unwary (among whom I count myself, certainly at the beginning of my career). A well-written, cogent minute by a junior member of the department is of little significance unless you can show it was acted upon further up the chain. Yet it would be wrong to dismiss the influence of officials entirely. It is true that on major issues of policy it is ministers who are responsible, and it is in the Cabinet and its committees that the big decisions are taken.[6] But such decisions are generally taken on the basis of advice offered by officials, and it is those same officials who sometimes define, and more often refine, those decisions and turn them into actions. Butterfield's mistrust of Vansittart, therefore, was not entirely misplaced.

Butterfield's second maxim – that there is a place for official history, but that it should be submitted to unremitting scrutiny – remains as valid today as it was in 1949. Official historians are still people 'to be shot at'. And his real thrust here is that academic history – history studied for its own sake and not for any imagined utility – must remain paramount and uncontaminated by any association with government. It is a belief to which, as we have seen, he remained faithful to the end of his life; and it is one worth bearing in mind in an era when academic historians are increasingly under pressure to demonstrate the impact of their research in the public sphere. We official historians have crossed the line and that is all very well,

---

[6] This is one of the two principal arguments made by Gill Bennett in her *Six Moments of Crisis: Inside British Foreign Policy* (Oxford, 2013). The other is that 'even in times of crisis, ministers always think about more than one issue, even if at the meeting in question they discuss a single issue' (p. 5).

for we have a useful function in serving up the materials that help unofficial historians to do their work. But we must still expect to be kept up to the mark. And if our contemporaries won't do that job, we can be sure that the ghost of Herbert Butterfield will always be there, taking pot shots at us with his rifle.

Appendix I

Herbert Butterfield on official history
Correspondence with Rev. A.W. Blaxall, April–May 1952[1]

1. Rev. A. W. Blaxall (Secretary/Treasurer, Christian Council of South Africa) to Butterfield, 6 April 1952

The Christian Council of South Africa
P.O. Box 81
Roodepoort
Transvaal

Dear Professor Butterfield,

It is perhaps presumptuous of a complete stranger to address you, and I shall understand if you do not have time to reply, although I hope otherwise.

You will understand that your book on History and Human Relations is particularly valuable for those of us who try to get the right perspective in a race conscious country like South Africa. The penultimate chapter has given me much to think about, especially because within recent months I have criticised our present Government who have appointed an historical research committee to write the real history of events which led to hostilities between the tiny Boer Republics and the mighty British Empire in 1899. The personnel of the committee include a few who will devote all their time to research, visiting countries overseas for the purpose, & others who will give part of their time. It is expected that the work will take *at least* five years, which means that salaries, overseas subsistence allowances, travelling expenses, together with the cost of clerical assistance, will run into scores of thousands of pounds – and that at a time when treasury is continually cutting down expenditure on social services on the ground of lack of funds. I wonder what you think about such costly research, especially when instigated by a Government which concentrates before all other things on building up what it is pleased to call the Afrikaner nation.

---

[1] BUTT/130/4. In 1963, already in his seventies, Blaxall was convicted of giving help to the banned African National Congress and Pan-Africanist Congress. He was imprisoned for a day and a night before being paroled and returning to Britain, where he died in 1970: see <https://www.sahistory.org.za/people/arthur-william-blaxall>.

May I conclude with a word of sincere thanks for the trouble you take to make your knowledge available to simple people, such as

Yours sincerely,
A.W. Blaxall

2. *Butterfield to Blaxall, 9 May 1952 (carbon copy)*

Dear Mr. Blaxall,

I am afraid that it is not easy for me to give a reply to your kind letter of 6 April, because so many complicated issues are involved; and it is necessary to know the whole situation and to catch the 'feel' of it before making a judgment.

I am personally very distrustful of official history, and I doubt very much whether in the long run any government will put down vast sums for any kind of history which operates to the detriment of the party or the people or the nation with which it feels its interests to be connected. Also I think that governments are not fit to direct the subjects to which large-scale historical research shall be turned in any given generation; though I cannot deny that there are topics on which a government might well feel that it could afford to allow everything to be known; and the financial support of government in such particular cases may serve the immediate objects of historical science itself.

I have noted (e.g. in the case of Ireland) that when a country is at a certain stage of its history, and when its historiography (or the organisation of its historical activities) is at a certain stage, there is a tendency for historians to look more particularly to the government for financial help, and that help may seem to answer so many purposes at the given moment that the tendency sometimes seems irresistible.

I personally am sceptical of the procedure even here, however, and have warned some of my Irish friends that at any rate I foresee difficulties in the future in respect of plans similar to the one which your letter describes. This kind of support on the part of the state may contribute something to the development of historical science at a given point in the story; but I think that it is going to have its dangers sooner or later.

I believe that most people would argue that some sort of support from the state has been necessary for the development of historical study everywhere, but of course there are other means by which the state could make its contribution (and even has made it in the past). I am sure that on a long-term view the ideal thing for historical study is a world of independent historians, choosing their own subjects for research, and allowed by the government free access to the archives.

In any case I believe that, though everybody may be well-intentioned in the first generation of government-organised history, there is actual evidence to confirm the view that with the passage of time further developments take place – what the state acquires innocuously in one generation becomes the starting-point, for a more serious encroachment in the next – and in the long run a momentous change is bound to take place in the relations between historians and the state. Clear evidence of the consequences of this are furnished in the case of a number of countries on the European continent even since 1919. Only the absolute independence of historians who are known to stand on their own footing can ensure in a given case that all the unpalatable truths will be allowed to come out. All the evils of any kind of official history become increased as the period which is being dealt with becomes more recent, i.e. approaches what we call 'contemporary history'.

The real reason why to some people it might seem quixotic to oppose these government projects is the fact that, in an age when the state is so clearly expanding its functions and multiplying its controls, the harnessing of historians to the state may be one of the inescapable tendencies of the time. I am not prepared to succumb to this argument, and I should always wish that if a government were to spend scores of thousands of pounds on history it would direct such expenditure in a way that took better care of the future and of the independence of historians. There are insidious pitfalls in the view that the independence of historians is adequately guarded in this kind of project, though sometimes it is not easy for the layman to see the pitfalls, and the historian who is involved in such projects comes to have a vested interest in them, so that he does not always seek to put himself into alliance with the independent outsider or to make the whole position clear. Sometimes also he gets a vested interest in a kind of 'orthodoxy' which has been established, so that the revision of historical versions and interpretations becomes more difficult. If it is only the official historians or officially-favoured historians who are allowed full access to the archives, they can clearly hamper any attempt to envisage a piece of history in a new framework. And if (as I have known to be the case) they get official support in attempts to put a check on the reviewing of their work, there is no possibility of their results really having to run the gauntlet of independent scholarship. There is no chance of any real criticism of an historical work if outsiders have no free access to the original documents; and I personally must hold reservations about all history written on periods or subjects for which the archives are not completely open. The one fight which historians have to make, therefore, is the fight for the opening of the archives; this is the real test of the genuineness of governmental patronage of historical study. I do not believe that if they are unopened (or partially unopened, or opened only to officially-favoured historians or to historians who can be penalised by withdrawal of salary) all the truth will be allowed to come out, as one project succeeds another.

Even in England, and still more in the U.S.A., the harnessing of scientists to the state has led to controversy, because some scientists believe that where the state controls the choice of topics and the direction which research is to take, extraneous motives are allowed to insert themselves – the free and balanced progress of science is hindered. I am sure that this argument applies *a fortiori* in the case of history, especially as concealed (and almost unconscious) motives of propaganda are liable to condition even the choice of the project to which the efforts of historians are to be directed.

It may be argued that a large co-operative undertaking is the most efficient way of securing a large-scale history within a reasonable time. I think that this is true only for history written at a certain level; it is true perhaps at a certain stage in the development of the historiography of a subject. It is all very well, provided, once the co-operative work is completed, the same archives are entirely open to the free play of scholarship, so that the enquiry can be carried to a further stage. The co-operative method (especially in the case of anything like an official history) often depends on the choice of a set of contributors who are united in the acceptance of a certain frame-work of reference, a certain over-all interpretation of the story. I have even known a case where a possible participant in such a venture was assured that he would be an 'independent historian' but was also told that of course it would be expected that he should conform to the accepted 'framework'.[2] All dangers in such organised enterprises are multiplied if there is likely to be any considerable motive for partiality on [*sic*] tendenciousness [*sic*] in the direction of it.

In any case the multiplicity of views and outlooks in a number of independent historians acting on an individualistic basis seems to me the necessary condition of progress in historical science, whereas co-operative and governmental endeavours tend to produce a kind of 'orthodoxy' which makes it more difficult for a new outlook or for unwelcome revelations to make their way in the world.

I remain,
Yours sincerely [unsigned]

---

[2] This sounds like Desmond Williams

3. Blaxall to Butterfield, 18 May 1952

Dear Prof. Butterfield,

This is merely to thank you most sincerely for your interesting, & important letter of the 9th. I expect to be in Cape Town shortly when I will see the Archbishop & tell him of our correspondence.

We are passing through a very difficult, and dark period in this country. It is extremely difficult to see how any semblance of democracy can be restored by constitutional means – the Christian Council is indeed fortunate in having Geoffrey Clayton as our president at this time.[3]

Again thanking you,

Very sincerely,
A.W. Blaxall

---

[3] Geoffrey Clayton was the Anglican Bishop of Johannesburg from 1934 to 1948 and Archbishop of Cape Town from 1948 until his death in 1957. He had been a Fellow and Dean of Peterhouse, 1910–14.

Appendix II

Cabinet Office Official Histories of the Second World War[1]

General Series

British War Economy, W.K. Hancock and M.M. Gowing (1949)
Problems of Social Policy, Richard M. Titmuss (1950)
British War Production, Michael M. Postan (1952)
Statistical Digest of the War, W.K. Hancock (1951)
Food, R.J. Hammond
    Volume I, *The Growth of Policy* (1951)
    Volume II, *Studies in Administration and Control* (1956)
    Volume III, *Studies in Administration and Control* (1962)
Agriculture, Keith A.H. Murray (1955)
The Economic Blockade, W.N. Medlicott
    Volume I (1952)
    Volume II (1959)
Merchant Shipping and the Demands of War, C.B.A. Behrens (1955)
Inland Transport, Christopher I. Savage (1957)
Financial Policy, 1939–45, Richard S. Sayers (1956)
Civil Industry and Trade, Eric L. Hargreaves (1952)
Manpower: Study of War-Time Policy and Administration, H.M.D. Parker (1957)
Oil: A Study of War-Time Policy and Administration, D.J. Payton-Smith (1971)
Coal, W.H.B. Court (1951)
Studies in the Social Services, Sheila Ferguson (1954)
Civil Defence, Terence H. O'Brien (1955)
Works and Buildings, Charles M. Kohan (1952)

War Production

The Administration of War Production, J.D. Scott (1955)
North American Supply, H. Duncan Hall (1955)
Studies of Overseas Supply, H. Duncan Hall (1956)
Contracts and Finance, William Ashworth (1953)

---

[1] Adapted from <http://www.ibiblio.org/hyperwar/UN/UK/index.html>. All volumes were published by HMSO unless otherwise stated.

Design and Development of Weapons: Studies in Government and Industrial Organisation, Michael M. Postan (1964)
The Control of Raw Materials, Joel Hurstfield (1953)
Labour in the Munitions Industries, P. Inman (1957)
Factories and Plant, William Hornby (1958)

Intelligence
British Intelligence in the Second World War, F.H. Hinsley et al.
    Volume I, *Its Influence on Strategy and Operations* (1979)
    Volume II, *Its Influence on Strategy and Operations* (1981)
    Volume III, Part 1, *Its Influence on Strategy and Operations* (1984)
    Volume III, Part 2, *Its Influence on Strategy and Operations* (1988)
    Volume IV, *Security and Counter-Intelligence* (1990)
    Volume V, *Strategic Deception*, Michael Howard (1990)
British Intelligence in the Second World War, Abridged Version, F.H. Hinsley et al. (1993)

Special Operations
SOE in France, Michael R.D. Foot (1966) (revised edition, Routledge, 2004)
SOE in the Low Countries, Michael R.D. Foot (St Ermin's Press, 2001)
SOE in the Far East, Charles Cruickshank (Oxford University Press, 1983)
SOE in Scandinavia, Charles Cruickshank (Oxford University Press, 1986)
Secret Flotillas, Brooks Richards (Frank Cass, 2004)
    Volume I, *Clandestine Sea Operations to Brittany 1940–1944*
    Volume II, *Clandestine Sea Operations in the Mediterranean, North Africa and the Adriatic 1940–1944*

Foreign Policy
British Foreign Policy in the Second World War, Abridged Version, Sir Llewellyn Woodward (1962)
British Foreign Policy in the Second World War, Sir Llewellyn Woodward
    Volume I (1970)
    Volume II (1971)
    Volume III (1971)
    Volume IV (1975)
    Volume V (1976)

Grand Strategy
Grand Strategy
    Volume I, *Rearmament Policy*, N.H. Gibbs (1976)

Volume II, *September 1939–June 1941*, J.R.M. Butler (1957)
Volume III, *Part 1: June 1941–August 1942*, J.M.A. Gwyer (1964)
Volume III, *Part 2: June 1941–August 1942*, J.R.M. Butler (1964)
Volume IV, *September 1942–August 1943*, Michael Howard (1970)
Volume V, *August 1943–September 1944*, John Ehrman (1956)
Volume VI, *October 1944–August 1945*, John Ehrman (1956)

Military Government
Civil Affairs and Military Government: Central Organization and Planning, Frank S.V. Donnison (1966)
Civil Affairs and Military Government: North-West Europe, 1944–1946, Frank S.V. Donnison (1961)
Allied Administration of Italy 1943–45, Charles R.S. Harris (1957)
British Military Administration in the Far East, 1943–1946, F.S.V. Donnison (1956)
British Military Administration of Occupied Territories in Africa During the Years 1941–1947, Lord Francis Rennell (1948)

The War at Sea
The War at Sea 1939–1945, S.W. Roskill
　　Volume I, *The Defensive* (1954)
　　Volume II, *The Period of Balance* (1956)
　　Volume III, *The Offensive, Part 1* (1960)
　　Volume III, *The Offensive, Part 2* (1961)

The War in the Air
The Strategic Air Offensive Against Germany, Sir Charles Webster and Noble Frankland
　　Volume I, *Preparation* (1961)
　　Volume II, *Endeavour* (1961)
　　Volume III, *Victory* (1961)
　　Volume IV, *Annexes and Appendices* (1961)

European Theatre
Defence of the United Kingdom, Basil Collier (1957)
The Campaign in Norway, T.K. Derry (1952)
The War in France and Flanders, 1939–1940, L.F. Ellis (1953)
Victory in the West
　　Volume I, *Battle of Normandy*, L.F. Ellis et al. (1962)
　　Volume II, *Victory in the West: Defeat of Germany*, L.F. Ellis et al. (1968)

Mediterranean, African and Middle East Theatres
The Mediterranean and Middle East

Volume I, *The Early Successes against Italy to May 1941*, I.S.O. Playfair et al. (1954)

Volume II, *The Germans Come to the Help of Their Ally, 1941* I.S.O. Playfair et al. (1956)

Volume III, *British Fortunes Reach Their Lowest Ebb*, I.S.O. Playfair et al. (1960)

Volume IV, *The Destruction of the Axis Forces in Africa*, I.S.O. Playfair, C.J.C. Molony et al. (1966)

Volume V, *The Campaign in Sicily, 1943, and the Campaign in Italy, 3rd September 1943 to 31st March 1944*, C.J.C. Molony (1973)

Volume VI, *Part 1: Victory in the Mediterranean: 1st April to 4th June 1944*, C.J.C. Molony (1984)

Volume VI, *Part 2: Victory in the Mediterranean: June to October 1944*, General Sir William Jackson et al. (1987)

Volume VI, *Part 3: Victory in the Mediterranean: November 1944 to May 1945*, General Sir William Jackson et al. (1988)

Asia-Pacific Theatres
The War against Japan, S. Woodburn Kirby et al.

Volume I, *The Loss of Singapore* (1957)

Volume II, *India's Most Dangerous Hour* (1958)

Volume III, *The Decisive Battles* (1961)

Volume IV, *The Reconquest of Burma* (1965)

Volume V, *The Surrender of Japan* (1969)

Appendix III

Cabinet Office Peacetime Official Histories[1]

The Nationalisation of British Industry, 1945–51, Sir Norman Chester (1975)

Environmental Planning, 1939–69, J.B. Cullingworth and G.E. Cherry (1975–81)
Volume I, *Reconstruction and Land Use Planning, 1939–1947*, J.B. Cullingworth (1975)
Volume II, *National Parks and Recreation in the Countryside*, Gordon E. Cherry (1975)
Volume III, *New Towns Policy*, J.B. Cullingworth (1979)
Volume IV, *Land Values, Compensation and Betterment*, J.B. Cullingworth (1981)

The Official History of Colonial Development, D.J. Morgan (Palgrave Macmillan, 1980)
Volume I, *The Origins of British Aid Policy, 1924–1945*
Volume II, *Developing British Colonial Resources, 1945–1951*
Volume III, *A Reassessment of British Aid Policy, 1951–1965*
Volume IV, *Changes in British Aid Policy, 1951–1970*
Volume V, *Guidance towards Self-Government in British Colonies, 1941–1971*

External Economic Policy since the War, L.S. Pressnell
Volume I, *The Post-War Financial Settlement* (1986)
Volume II (Frank Cass, 2002) (?)[2]

---

[1] Compiled from the sources given on p. 53, note 38, and from various library and publishers' catalogues. There may still be some inaccuracies (particularly regarding publication dates) but (I hope) no omissions. With one exception (*Colonial Development*) all volumes from 1975 to 1995 were published by HMSO; volumes dated 2002 were published by Frank Cass and all volumes from 2005 onwards by Routledge.

[2] I have been unable to locate any reference to this second volume apart from the date (given elsewhere as 2005) and publisher. In 2008 the Cabinet Office described this volume as being 'in preparation'. According to Professor Pressnell's obituary (*The Times*, 29 September 2011), 'His talents as an economist and a historian came to the fore when he was commissioned by the Cabinet Office to write a government official history on Britain's external economic policy since the Second World War. The first volume – *The Post-War Financial Settlement* – appeared in 1986, and the second was still in progress at his death.' So I assume that the volume does not in fact exist.

The Health Services since the War, Charles Webster
  Volume I, *Problems of Health Care: The National Health Service before 1957* (1988)
  Volume II, *Government and Health Care: The British National Health Service 1958–1979* (1996)

The Official History of the British Part in the Korean War, General Sir Anthony Farrar-Hockley
  Volume I, *A Distant Obligation* (1990)
  Volume II, *An Honourable Discharge* (1995)

The Official History of Britain and the European Community
  Volume I, *The Rise and Fall of a National Strategy, 1945–1963*, Alan S. Milward (2002)
  Volume II, *From Rejection to Referendum, 1963–1975*, Sir Stephen Wall (2013)
  Volume III, *The Tiger Unleashed, 1975–1985*, Sir Stephen Wall (2018)

The Official History of the Falklands Campaign, Sir Lawrence Freedman (2005)
  Volume I, *The Origins of the Falklands War*
  Volume II, *War and Diplomacy*

The Official History of Britain and the Channel Tunnel, Terry Gourvish (2006)

The Official History of Privatisation, David Parker (2009)
  Volume I, *The Formative Years 1970–1987*
  Volume II, *Popular Capitalism 1987–1997*

The Official History of North Sea Oil and Gas, Alex Kemp (2014)
  Volume I, *The Growing Dominance of the State*
  Volume II, *Moderating the State's Role*

The Official History of the British Civil Service, Rodney Lowe and Hugh Pemberton
  Reforming the Civil Service, Volume I, *The Fulton Years, 1966–81*, Rodney Lowe (2011)
  Reforming the Civil Service, Volume II, *The Thatcher and Major Revolutions, 1982–97*, Rodney Lowe and Hugh Pemberton (2020)

The Official History of the Joint Intelligence Committee, Michael Goodman
  Volume I, *From the Approach of the Second World War to the Suez Crisis* (2014)
  Volume II [in preparation]

The Official History of the UK Strategic Nuclear Deterrent, Matthew Jones (2017)
  Volume I, *From the V-Bomber Era to the Arrival of Polaris, 1945–1964*
  Volume II, *The Labour Government and the Polaris Programme, 1964–1970*

The Official History of Criminal Justice in England and Wales, Paul Rock and David Downes
  Volume I, *The 'Liberal Hour'*, Paul Rock (2019)
  Volume II, *Institution-Building*, Paul Rock (2019)
  Volume III, *The Rise and Fall of Penal Hope*, David Downes (2021)

Official histories commissioned outside the regular series

Churchill's Man of Mystery: Desmond Morton and the World of Intelligence, Gill Bennett (2007)
Secrecy and the Media: The Official History of the United Kingdom's D-Notice System, Nick Wilkinson (2009)
The Official History of the Cabinet Secretaries, Ian Beesley (2018)

Appendix IV

Foreign Office Documentary Series[1]

British Documents on the Origins of the War, 1898–1914 (BD)

Editors: G.P. Gooch and H.W.V. Temperley (vols I–X), Sir J. Headlam-Morley (vol. XI)

    I. The End of British Isolation (1927)
   II. The Anglo-Japanese Alliance and the Franco-British Entente (1927)
  III. The Testing of the Entente 1904–6 (1928)
  IV. The Anglo-Russian Rapprochement 1903–7 (1929)
   V. The Macedonian Problem and the Annexation of Bosnia 1903–9 (1928)
  VI. Anglo-German Tension 1907–12 (1930)
 VII. The Agadir Crisis (1932)
VIII. Arbitration, Neutrality and Security (1932)
  IX. The Balkan Wars: Part I: The Prelude; The Tripoli War (1933)
       The Balkan Wars: Part II: The League and Turkey (1934)
   X. Part I: The Near and Middle East on the Eve of War (1936)
       Part II: The Last Years of Peace (1938)
  XI. The Outbreak of War (1926)

Documents on British Foreign Policy, 1919–1939 (DBFP)

Editors: Professor E.L. Woodward, Dr R. Butler, Mr J.P.T. Bury, Professor W.N. Medlicott, Professor D. Dakin and Miss M.E. Lambert (Mrs M.E. Pelly).

First Series (1919–25)

    I. Proceedings of the Supreme Council July–October 1919 (1947)
   II. Proceedings of the Supreme Council October 1919–January 1920. Meetings in London and Paris of Allied Ministers December 1919–January 1920 (1948)

---

[1] Source: FCO Historians, *History at the Heart of Diplomacy*, pp. 104–10, <https://issuu.com/fcohistorians/docs/history_at_the_heart_of_diplomacy-w>, with later additions.

III. Withdrawal of German Forces from the Baltic Provinces July–December 1919. Policy of HMG with regard to Russia, May 1919–March 1920. Eastern Galicia, June–December 1919 (1949)

IV. Adriatic and the Near East 1919–February 1920 (1952)

V. Western Europe, June 1919–January 1920 and Viscount Grey's mission to Washington, August–December 1919 (1954)

VI. Central Europe, June 1919–January 1920 and HMG's Relations with Japan, June 1919–April 1920 (1956)

VII. First Conference of London, February–April 1920 (1958)

VIII. Conversations and Conferences, 1920 (1958)

IX. German Affairs, 1920 (1960)

X. German Affairs and Plebiscites, 1920 (1960)

XI. Plebiscite in Upper Silesia, January 1920–March 1921, and Poland, Danzig and the Baltic States, January 1920–March 1921 (1960)

XII. Western and Central Europe and the Balkan States, 1920; Transcaucasia and Russia, February 1920–March 1921 (1962)

XIII. Near East, February 1920–March 1921 (1963)

XIV. Far Eastern Affairs 1920–22 (1966)

XV. International Conferences and Conversations 1921 (1967)

XVI. Upper Silesia 1921–2 and Germany 1921 (1968)

XVII. Greece and Turkey 1921–22 (1970)

XVIII. Greece and Turkey 1922–23 (1972)

XIX. The Conferences of Cannes, Genoa and the Hague 1922 (1974)

XX. German Reparations and Allied Military Control 1922 and Russia, March 1921–December 1922 (1976)

XXI. German Reparations and Military Control 1923 (1978)

XXII. Central Europe and the Balkans 1921 and Albania 1921–2 (1980)

XXIII. Poland and the Balkan states 1921–23 (1981)

XXIV. Anglo-Italian Conversations 1922 and Central Europe and the Balkans 1922–23 (1983)

XXV. Russia 1923–25 and the Baltic States 1924–25 (1984)

XXVI. Central Europe and the Balkans; German Reparation and Allied Military Control, 1924 (1985)

XXVII. Germany 1925 and the Locarno Treaty (1986)

Series IA (1925–30)

I. The Aftermath of Locarno 1925–26 (1966)

II. The Termination of Military Control in Germany and Middle East and American Questions 1926–27 (1968)

III. European and Naval Questions 1922 (1970)

   IV. European and Security Questions 1927–28 (1971)

    V. European and Security Questions 1928 (1973)

   VI. The Young Report and the Hague Conference: Security Questions 1928–29 (1975)

  VII. German, Austrian and Middle East Questions 1929–30 (1975)

Second Series (1929–38)

     I. London Naval Conference and European Affairs 1929–31 (1946)

    II. Austrian and German Affairs and the World Monetary Crisis 1931 (1947)

   III. Reparations and Disarmament 1931–32 (1948)

   IV. The Disarmament Conference and the Internal Situation in Germany 1932–33 (1950)

    V. European Affairs and War Debts March–October 1933 (1956)

   VI. European Affairs and War Debts October 1933–August 1934 (1957)

  VII. Anglo-Soviet Relations 1929–34 (1958)

 VIII. Chinese Affairs and Japanese Action in Manchuria 1929–31 (1960)

   IX. The Far Eastern Crisis 1931–32 (1965)

    X. Far Eastern Affairs March–October 1932 (1969)

   XI. Far Eastern Affairs October 1932–June 1933 (1970)

  XII. European Affairs August 1934–April 1935 (1972)

 XIII. Naval Policy and Defence Requirements July 1934–March 1936 (1973)

 XIV. The Italo-Ethiopian Dispute March 1934–October 1935 (1976)

  XV. The Italo-Ethiopian War and German Affairs October 1935–February 1936 (1976)

 XVI. The Rhineland Crisis and the Ending of Sanctions March–July 1936 (1977)

XVII. Western Pact Negotiations: Outbreak of Spanish Civil War, June 1936–January 1937 (1979)

XVIII. European Affairs, January–June 1937 (1980)

 XIX. European Affairs, July 1937–August 1938 (1982)

  XX. Far Eastern Affairs, May 1933–November 1936 (1984)

 XXI. Far Eastern Affairs, November 1936–July 1938 (1984)

Third Series (1938–1939)

    I. The German Invasion of Austria and the First Phase of the Czechoslovak Crisis, March–July 1938 (1949)

   II. The Development of the Czechoslovak Crisis from the Runciman

Mission to the Munich Conference, July–September 1938 (1949)

III. Polish and Hungarian Claims on Czechoslovak Territory; The Enforcement by Germany of the Munich Agreement; Anglo-Italian Relations: September 1938–January 1939 (1950)

IV. Hopes of General European Appeasement Abandoned; Attempts Are Made to Form a 'Common Front' against Further German Aggression, January–April 1939 (1951)

V. Increasing German Threats to Poland and British Efforts to Create a Common Front against Further German and Italian Aggression, April–June 1939 (1952)

VI. An Important Phase in Anglo-Franco-Soviet negotiations; Anglo-Turkish Negotiations; and the German Menace to Poland, June–August 1939 (1953)

VII. Unsuccessful Attempts to Deter Germany from Aggression against Poland; Diplomatic Exchanges Immediately Preceding the British Declaration of War on Germany, August–September 1939 (1954)

VIII. Policy in the Far East; Attitude of HMG towards the Sino-Japanese Conflict; Interaction of Events in the Far East and Western Europe, August 1938–April 1939 (1955).

IX. Policy in the Far East during the Five Months Preceding the Outbreak of War in Europe, April–September 1939 (1955)

X. Index (1961)

Documents on British Policy Overseas, 1945– (DBPO)

Editors: Dr R. Butler, Mrs M.E. Pelly, Dr R. Bullen, Mrs H.J. Yasamee, Ms G. Bennett, Dr K.A. Hamilton, Dr S.R. Ashton, Professor P. Salmon, Dr S. Twigge, Dr R. Smith, Dr T. Insall, Dr I. Tombs.

Series I (1945–50)

I. The Conference at Potsdam, July–August 1945 (1984)

II. Conferences and Conversations 1945: London, Washington and Moscow (1985)

III. Britain and America: Negotiation of the United States Loan, August–December 1945 (1986)

IV. Britain and America: Atomic Energy, Bases and Food, December 1945–July 1946 (1987)

V. Germany and Western Europe, August–December 1945 (1990)

VI. Eastern Europe, August 1945–April 1946 (1991)

VII. The United Nations: Iran, Cold War and World Organisation, January 1946–January 1947 (1995)
VIII. Britain and China, 1945–1950 (2002)
IX. The Nordic Countries: From War to Cold War, 1944–1951 (2011)
X. The Brussels and North Atlantic Treaties, 1947–51 (2015)
XI. European Recovery and the Search for Western Security, 1946–48 (2016)

Series II (1950–5)

I. The Schuman Plan, the Council of Europe and Western European Integration, May 1950–December 1952 (1986)
II. The London Conferences, January–June 1950 (1987)
III. German Rearmament, September–December 1950 (1989)
IV. Korea, June 1950–April 1951 (1991)

Series III (1960–)

I. Britain and the Soviet Union, 1968–1972 (1997)
II. The Conference on Security and Co-operation in Europe, 1972–1975 (1997)
III. Détente in Europe, 1972–1976 (2001)
IV. The Year of Europe: America, Europe and the Energy Crisis, 1972–1974 (2006)
V. The Southern Flank in Crisis, 1973–1976 (2006)
VI. Berlin in the Cold War, 1948–1990 (2009)
VII. German Unification, 1989–1990 (2009)
VIII. The Invasion of Afghanistan and UK–Soviet Relations, 1979–82 (2012)
IX. The Challenge of Apartheid: UK–South African Relations, 1985–1986 (2016)
X. The Polish Crisis and Relations with Eastern Europe, 1979–1982 (2017)
XI. The Unwinding of Apartheid: UK–South African Relations, 1986–1990 (2019)
XII. Britain and the Revolutions in Eastern Europe, 1989 (2020)

Bibliography

Unpublished primary sources

Private papers

Sir Herbert Butterfield (Cambridge University Library)

BUTT/52	Foreign historians, 1945–1949
BUTT/53	Foreign historians, 1950–1959
BUTT/54	Foreign historians, 1960–1969
BUTT/57	Geyl, Schramm and Ritter, 1951–1967
BUTT/130	Official history, 1945–1954
BUTT/531/W	Correspondence with Desmond Williams

The Hon. Margaret Lambert (private collection, consulted by permission of Sophia Lambert).

Official papers

The National Archives (TNA), London:

FO 370/2906   Library and Research Department General Correspondence: Implications of government proposal that official histories be extended to cover peacetime (1966).

Foreign, Commonwealth and Development Office (FCDO), London:

FCO Historians' collection: Miscellaneous working papers.

Published primary sources

Akten zur Auswärtigen Politik der Bundesrepublik Deutschland (AAPD)
(Berlin, 1997–).

Bennett, Gill, and Richard Smith (eds), *Britain and the Making of the
Post-War World: The Potsdam Conference and Beyond* (2020), https://
issuu.com/fcohistorians/docs/britain_and_the_making_of_the_post-
war_world_with; https://www.amazon.co.uk/Britain-making-Post-
War-World-Conference/dp/B08CWCGSNR.

British Documents on the End of Empire (BDEEP) (16 vols, London,
1992–2006), https://bdeep.org/.

British Documents on the Origins of the War 1898–1914 (BD) (11 vols,
London, 1926–38).

Cabinet Office, *The UK Government's Official Histories Programme*
(2008), https://webarchive.nationalarchives.gov.uk/20080205143007/
http://www.cabinetoffice.gov.uk/publicationscheme/published_
information/1/officialhistory.aspx.

Die Grosse Politik der europäischen Kabinette 1871–1914 (GP) (54 vols,
Berlin, 1922–7).

Diplomatic Documents of Switzerland (Berne, 1979–).

Documents on British Foreign Policy 1919–1939 (DBFP) (64 vols, London,
1947–86).

Documents on British Policy Overseas (DBPO) (London, Abingdon, 1984–).

Documents on German Foreign Policy 1918–1945 (DGFP), Series C:
1933–1937 (6 vols, London and Washington, DC, 1957–83); Series D:
1937–1941 (13 vols, London and Washington, DC, 1949–64).

Documents on Irish Policy (Dublin, 1997–).

Foreign Relations of the United States (FRUS) (Washington, DC, 1861–).

House of Lords Hansard, vol. 698, 5 February 2008, cols. 1013–25; vol. 747,
10 July 2013, cols. 335–51; vol. 767, 30 December 2015, cols. 189–200.

House of Lords Library, research briefing: 'The UK Government's Official
Histories Programme' (2015), https://lordslibrary.parliament.uk/
research-briefings/lif-2015-0056/.

Opsahl, Erik (ed.), *Arne Ordings dagbøker*, bind I, *19. juni 1942–23. juli
1945* (Oslo, 2000).

Pilling, Sir Joe, Review of the Government's Official History Programme (2009), https://assets.publishing.service.gov.uk/government/uploads/system/uploads/attachment_data/file/62233/future-plans-government.pdf.

Polish Diplomatic Documents (Warsaw, 2005–).

Sontag, Raymond J., and James Stuart Beddie (eds), *Nazi–Soviet Relations 1939–1941* (Washington, DC, 1948) https://avalon.law.yale.edu/subject_menus/nazsov.asp.

UK Parliament, Members and Lords: Lord Rodgers of Quarry Bank, Written Questions (9 July 2019), https://members.parliament.uk/member/940/writtenquestions#expand-1137959.

Wilson, Harold, Memorandum, 'The Fifty-Year Rule', 27 July 1965, printed in Keith Wilson, *Forging the Collective Memory: Government and International Historians through Two World Wars* (Providence, RI, and Oxford, 1996), pp. 289–93.

Secondary works

Aldrich, Richard J., 'Policing the Past: Official History, Secrecy and British Intelligence Since 1945', *English Historical Review* 119, 483 (Sept. 2004), pp. 922–53.

Annan, Noel, *Our Age: Portrait of a Generation* (London, 1990).

Beck, Peter J. 'Locked in a Dusty cupboard, neither accessible on the policy-makers' desks nor cleared for early publication: Llewellyn Woodward's official diplomatic history of the Second World War', *English Historical Review*, cxxvii (2012), 1435–70.

Behrens, C.B.A., *Merchant Shipping and the Demands of War* (London, 1955).

Bennett, Gill, *Six Moments of Crisis: Inside British Foreign Policy* (Oxford, 2013).

Bennett, Gill, *The Zinoviev Letter: The Conspiracy that Never Dies* (Oxford, 2018).

Bentley, Michael, 'Herbert Butterfield and the ethics of historiography', *History and Theory*, xliv (Feb. 2005), 55–71.

Bentley, Michael, *The Life and Thought of Herbert Butterfield: History, Science and God* (Cambridge, 2011).

Bialer, Uri, 'Telling the truth to the people: Britain's decision to publish the diplomatic papers of the inter-war period', *Historical Journal*, xxvi (Jun.1983), 349–67.

Black, Jeremy, and Karl Schweizer, 'the value of diplomatic history: A case study in the thought of Herbert Butterfield', *Diplomacy and Statecraft*, xvii (2006), 617–31.

Bloch, Michael, *Operation Willi: The Plot to Kidnap the Duke of Windsor, July 1940* (London, 1984).

Breuning, Eleanor, 'International cooperation', in *Papers Presented at the Seminar for Editors of Diplomatic Documents, Held in the Foreign and Commonwealth Office on 9 November 1989* (Occasional Papers No. 2, London, 1989), pp. 39–43.

Burk, Kathleen, *Troublemaker: The Life and History of A.J.P. Taylor* (New Haven and London, 2000).

Butterfield, Herbert, *Christianity and History* (London, 1949).

Butterfield, Herbert, *George III, Lord North and the People, 1779–80* (London, 1949).

Butterfield, Herbert, *History and Human Relations* (London, 1951).

Butterfield, Herbert, *Man on His Past: The Study of the History of Historical Scholarship* (Cambridge, 1955).

Butterfield, Herbert, 'Official history: Its pitfalls and its criteria', *Studies: An Irish Quarterly Review*, xxxviii (June 1949), 129–44.

Butterfield, Herbert, *The Origins of Modern Science 1300–1800* (London, 1949).

Butterfield, Herbert, *The Peace Tactics of Napoleon, 1806–1809* (Cambridge, 1929).

Butterfield, Herbert, 'Tendencies in historical study in England', *Irish Historical Studies*, iv (Mar. 1945), 209–223.

Butterfield, Herbert, *The Whig Interpretation of History* (London, 1931).

Cannon, John, 'Butterfield, Herbert', in John Cannon et al. (eds), *The Blackwell Dictionary of Historians* (Oxford, 1988), pp. 61–2.

Cloake, John, 'The scholar cadet: More recollections of Peterhouse in the 1940s', *Peterhouse Annual Record 2003/2004*, pp. 13–25.

Cowling, Maurice, 'Herbert Butterfield, 1900–1979', *Proceedings of the British Academy*, lxv (1979), 595–609.

Cox, Seb, 'Setting the historical agenda: Webster and Frankland and the debate over the strategic bombing offensive against Germany, 1939–1945', in *The Last Word: Essays on Official History in the United States and the British Commonwealth*, ed. Jeffrey Grey (Westport, CT, and London, 2003), pp. 147–73.

Cruickshank, Charles, *SOE in the Far East* (Oxford, 1983).

Cruickshank, Charles, *SOE in Scandinavia* (Oxford, 1986).

Dahl, Hans Fredrik, *Quisling: A Study in Treachery* (Cambridge, 1999).

Davenport-Hines, Richard, and Adam Sisman (eds), *One Hundred Letters from Hugh Trevor-Roper* (Oxford, 2014).

Davies, Peter, *British Defence Economic Intelligence: A Cold War in Whitehall 1929–90* (2019).

Derry, John, 'Herbert Butterfield', in *The Historian at Work*, ed. John Cannon (London, 1980), pp. 171–87.

Eckert, Astrid M., *The Struggle for the Files: The Western Allies and the Return of German Archives after the Second World War* (New York, 2012).

Elton, G.R., 'Herbert Butterfield and the study of history', *Historical Journal*, xxvii (1984), 729–43.

Eyck, Frank, *G.P. Gooch: A Study in History and Politics* (London and Basingstoke, 1982).

FCO Historians, *History at the Heart of Diplomacy: Historians in the Foreign Office, 1918–2018* (History Note No. 22, London 2018), https://issuu.com/fcohistorians/docs/history_at_the_heart_of_diplomacy-w.

FCO Historians, *Nazi Gold: Information from the British Archives* (History Note No. 11, London, 1996), https://issuu.com/fcohistorians/docs/history_notes_cover_hphn_11.

FCO Historians, *Nazi Gold: Part II: Information from the British Archives* (History Note No. 12, London, 1997), https://issuu.com/fcohistorians/docs/history_notes_cover_hphn_12.

FCO Historical Branch, *Papers Presented at the Seminar 'Valid Evidence', Held in the FCO Library Cornwall House, on 6 November 1987* (Occasional Papers No. 1, London, 1987), https://issuu.com/fcohistorians/docs/hpop_1.

FCO Historical Branch, *Papers Presented at the Seminar for Editors of*

Diplomatic Documents, Held in the Foreign and Commonwealth Office on 9 November 1989 (Occasional Papers No. 2, London, 1989).

Frankland, Noble, *History at War* (London, 1998).

Gowing, Margaret, *Britain and Atomic Energy, 1939–1945* (London, 1964).

Gowing, Margaret, and Lorna Arnold, *Independence and Deterrence: Britain and Atomic Energy, 1945–52* (2 vols, London, 1974).

Grant, Matthew, 'History and policy', in *A Practical Guide to Studying History: Skills and Approaches*, ed. Tracey Loughran (London, 2017), pp. 233–47.

Hamilton, Keith, *Transformational Diplomacy after the Cold War: Britain's Know How Fund in Post-Communist Europe, 1989–2003* (London and New York, 2013).

Hancock, W.K., *Country and Calling* (London, 1954).

Hancock, W.K., and M.M. Gowing, *British War Economy* (London, 1949).

Harris, Jose, 'Thucydides amongst the mandarins: Hancock and the World War II civil histories', in *Keith Hancock: The Legacies of an Historian*, ed. D.A. Low (Carlton, Victoria, 2001), pp. 122–48.

Hayton, David, *Conservative Revolutionary: The Lives of Lewis Namier* (Manchester, 2019).

Heuston, R.F.V., review of *War Crimes Trials*, vols 4 and 5 (*The Hadamar and Natzweiler Trials*, London, 1949) and *Law Reports of Trials of War Criminals*, vols 10–13 (London, 1949), *International Law Quarterly*, iii (Apr. 1950), 307–9.

Jones, Matthew, *The Official History of the UK Strategic Nuclear Deterrent* (2 vols, London, 2017).

Kent, George O., 'Editing diplomatic documents: A review of official US and German document series', *American Archivist*, lvii (1994), 462–81.

Kent, George O., 'The German Foreign Ministry's archives at Whaddon Hall, 1948–58', *American Archivist*, xxiv (1961), 43–54.

Keogh, Dermot, *Ireland and Europe 1919–1948* (Dublin and Totowa, NJ, 1988).

Lammers, Donald, 'From Whitehall after Munich: The Foreign Office and the future course of British policy', *Historical Journal*, xvi (1973), 831–56.

Lowe, Rodney, 'Official history', https://archives.history.ac.uk/makinghistory/resources/articles/official_history.html.

McGuire, James, 'T. Desmond Williams (1921–87)', *Irish Historical Studies*, xxvi (May 1988), 3–7.

McIntire, C.T., *Herbert Butterfield: Historian as Dissenter* (New Haven and London, 2004).

Medlicott, W.N., *The Economic Blockade* (2 vols, London, 1952–9).

Mehta, Ved, *Fly and the Fly Bottle: Encounters with British Intellectuals* (London, 1961).

Moore, Charles, *Margaret Thatcher: The Authorized Biography*, vol. 2, *Everything She Wants* (London, 2015).

Murphy, Christopher J., 'The origins of *SOE in France*', *Historical Journal*, xlvi (2003), 935–52.

Namier, L.B., *Diplomatic Prelude 1938–1939* (London, 1948).

Namier, L.B., *Europe in Decay 1936–1940* (London, 1950).

Noack, Ulrich, biographical details: *Universität Greifswald im Nationalsozialismus*, https://ns-zeit.uni-greifswald.de/projekt/personen/noack-ulrich/.

Pelly, Margaret, 'Sensitive documents and editorial freedom', in FCO Historians, *Papers Presented at the Seminar for Editors of Diplomatic Documents, Held in the Foreign and Commonwealth Office on 9 November 1989* (Occasional Papers No. 2, London, 1989), pp. 44–7.

Postan, Michael M., *British War Production* (London, 1952).

Riste, Olav, 'Open season for rewriting history', *The Times*, 10 June 1986, p. 12.

Sato, Shohei, '"Operation Legacy": Britain's destruction and concealment of colonial records worldwide', *Journal of Imperial and Commonwealth History*, xlv, 697–719.

Seldon, Anthony, 'Why every government department needs a resident historian', *Prospect*, 1 May 2020, https://www.prospectmagazine.co.uk/politics/government-department-chief-historian-whitehall-number-10-coronavirus-covid-brexit.

Sharp, Paul, 'Herbert Butterfield, the English School and the civilizing virtues of diplomacy', *International Affairs*, lxxix (Jul. 2003), 855–78.

Simms, Brendan, 'Butterfield, Sir Herbert (1900–1979)', *Oxford Dictionary of National Biography*, https://doi.org/10.1093/ref:odnb/30888.

Spencer, Frank, 'The publication of British and German diplomatic documents for the period of the inter-war years', *History*, xlvii (1962), 254–86.

Svendsen, Åsmund, *Halvdan Koht. Veien mot framtiden. En biografi* (Oslo, 2013).

Sweet, Paul R., 'Der Versuch amtlicher Einflussnahme auf die Edition der "Documents on German Foreign Policy, 1933–1941". Ein Fall aus den fünfziger Jahren', *Vierteljahrshefte für Zeitgeschichte*, xxxix (Apr. 1991), 265–303.

Sweet, Paul R., 'The Windsor File', *The Historian*, lix (1997), 263–79.

Taylor, A.J.P., *English History 1914–1945* (Oxford, 1965; revised paperback edition, Harmondsworth, 1970).

Taylor, A.J.P., *A Personal History* (London, 1984; paperback edition, 1984).

Taylor, A.J.P., Review of Charles Tansill, *Back Door to War: Roosevelt's Foreign Policy 1933–1941*, *Manchester Guardian*, 24 October 1952, reprinted as 'Roosevelt and the War', in *Struggles for Supremacy*, ed. Wrigley, pp. 245–7.

Taylor, A.J.P., *The Origins of the Second World War* (London, 1961).

Taylor, A.J.P., *The Struggle for Mastery in Europe 1848–1918* (Oxford, 1954).

Wall, Stephen, *The Official History of Britain and the European Community*, vol. 3 (2018).

Watt, D. Cameron, 'British historians, the war guilt issue, and post-war Germanophobia: A documentary note', *Historical Journal*, xxxvi (1993), 179–85.

Weinberg, Gerhard L., 'Critical note on the *Documents on German Foreign Policy, 1918–1945*', *Journal of Modern History*, xxiii (1951), 38–40.

Welch, Colin, *Daily Telegraph* obituary of 1 February 1997, reprinted in *Peterhouse Annual Record 2011/2012* (Cambridge, 2016), pp. 116–19.

Wheeler-Bennett, Sir John, *Friends, Enemies and Sovereigns* (London, 1976).

Williams, T. Desmond, 'The historiography of World War II', in *Historical Studies* I, ed. T. Desmond Williams (London, 1958), pp. 33–49; reprinted in. *The Origins of the Second World War: Historical Interpretations*, ed. Esmonde M. Robertson (London and Basingstoke, 1971), pp. 36–64.

Williams, T. Desmond, 'Some aspects of contemporary history', *Cambridge Journal*, ii (Sept. 1949), 733–42.

Wilson, Keith, 'Introduction: Governments, historians, and "historical engineering"', in *Forging the Collective Memory: Governments and International Relations Through Two World Wars*, ed. Keith Wilson (Providence, RI, and London, 1996), pp. 1–27.

Wilson, S.S., *The Cabinet Office to 1945* (Public Records Handbook No. 17, London, 1975).

Woodward, E.L., 'Some considerations on the present state of historical studies', *Proceedings of the British Academy 1950*, 95–112.

Woodward, E.L., *The Study of International Relations at a University: An Inaugural Lecture Delivered before the University of Oxford on 17 February 1945* (Oxford, 1945).

Woodward, Sir Llewellyn, *British Foreign Policy in the Second World War* (5 vols, London, 1970–6).

Wrigley, Chris (ed.), *Struggles for Supremacy: Diplomatic Essays by A.J.P. Taylor* (Aldershot, 2000).

Zala, Sacha, *Geschichte unter der Schere politischer Zensur. Amtliche Aktensammlungen im internationalen Vergleich* (Munich, 2001).

Index

Acton, Lord, 10n, 36
Admiralty, 36
Afghanistan, 63
Air Ministry, 35–6
Akten zur Auswärtigen Politik der Bundesrepublik Deutschland (AAPD), 50n, 64n
Aldrich, Richard, 2
All Souls College, Oxford, 5–6
Andrew, Christopher, 57
  Defence of the Realm, 57
Anglo-French Soviet negotiations (1939), 31
Annan, Noel, 42
Anschluss, German-Austrian (1938), 6
Auslandsorganisation (of Nazi Party), 10
Austria, 8n, 11, 37
Bahamas, 18
Baumont, Maurice, 11n
Behrens, Betty, 4–5
Bennett, Gill, 59–62, 67n
Bentley, Michael, 1–2, 5, 34, 40
Berlin, 7, 9–11, 19
Bevin, Ernest, 10, 19, 26
Bew, John, 62
Bew, Lord (Paul), 55
Blaxall, Rev A.W., 43n, 69–73
Bletchley Park, 3, 7
Boer War (1899–1902), 69
Bonn, 49
Brexit, 63
Bridges, Sir Edward, 54n
British Academy, 41, 43
British Broadcasting Corporation (BBC), 1
British Documents on the End of Empire (BDEEP), 52n
British Documents on the Origins of the War 1898–1914 (BD), 5, 35, 37, 39, 50n, 61
Brook, Sir Norman, 47
Bullen, Roger, 58–9
Bury, Patrick, 25, 47
Butler (Sir) James (J.R.M.), 4, 32n, 45, 48
Butler, Rohan, 6, 14, 19, 43, 47, 51–2, 57–8, 61
Butterfield, (Sir) Herbert, ix–xi
  academic career, 1, 41
  and German historians, 7, 10n
  and official historians, 1–8, 25–33
  and official history, 1–8, 33–40, 43–5, 64–73
  and Harold Temperley, ix–xi, 3, 5, 6, 8, 34–5, 41
  and Desmond Williams, ix–xi, 8–13, 15–22, 32–33, 42–4
  Christianity and History, 1, 41
  George III, Lord North and the People, 1
  History and Human Relations, viii, 2, 19–20, 23–4, 33, 37, 43, 69
  Man on His Past, viii, 37
  'Official history: Its pitfalls and criteria' (1951), viii, 1–3, 24, 33–34, 36–40
  'Official history: Its pitfalls and its criteria' (1949), xi, 1–3, 13–16, 18, 21–3, 25, 32–4, 36–7, 39, 44
  The Origins of Modern Science 1300–1800, 1
  The Peace Tactics of Napoleon, 1806–1809, x, 35
  The Whig Interpretation of History, x
Cabinet Office, xi, 4, 26, 28, 51, 53–7, 62–3. *See also Official History of the*

Second World War; Peacetime Official Histories
Historical Section, 51
Histories, Openness and Records Unit, 53–4
Cabinet Secretary, 47, 54, 54n, 56, 62
Cabinet, 67
minutes, publication of, 29–30
Cambridge Historical Journal, 1
Cambridge Journal, 33
Cambridge, 9, 16
Cambridge, University of, 1, 4–5, 8–9, 17, 35, 41–2
Divinity School, 12
Cameron, David, 47
Cannadine, Sir David, 63
Canning, George, 14
Cannon, John, 41
Cape Town, 73
Carroll, Malcolm, 20
Case, Simon, 62
Chamberlain, Neville, 9, 62
Cherry, G.E., 53
Environmental Planning, 1939–69 (with J.B. Cullingworth), 53
Chester, Sir Norman, 53
The Nationalisation of British Industry, 1945–51, 53
Chilcot Inquiry, 63
Churchill, Winston, 22
Clark, Grahame, 36
Clayton, Geoffrey, 73
Cold War, 10, 57, 59, 61
Colonial Office, 52
Common Market (EEC), 52
Commonwealth Office, 52
Commonwealth Relations Office, 52
Connolly, Father P.J., SJ, 13–14
Corpus Christi College, Cambridge, 25
Cowling, Maurice, 41–2
Crawley, Charles, 8n
Cruickshank, Charles, 52
SOE in France, 52

SOE in Scandinavia, 52
Cullingworth, J.B., 53
Environmental Planning, 1939–69 (with G.E. Cherry), 53
Dacre, Lord. *See* Trevor-Roper, Hugh
Dakin, Douglas, 47
Department of Transport, 57
Derry, T.K., 46
The Campaign in Norway, 46
Diplomatic Documents of Switzerland, 61
Documenti Diplomatici Italiani, I, 64n
Documenti sulla Politica Internazionale dell'Italia, 64n
Documents on British Foreign Policy 1919–1939 (DBFP), 6, 13–16, 20, 25–32, 38, 45, 47–9, 57, 61
Documents on British Policy Overseas (DBPO), 57–62
Berlin in the Cold War 1948–1990, 60
Britain and the Soviet Union, 1968–1972, 60
The Conference at Potsdam, July–August 1945, 58
The Conference on Security and Cooperation in Europe 1972–1975, 60
Détente in Europe 1972–1976, 60
The Year of Europe: America, Europe and the Energy Crisis 1972–1974, 60
Documents on German Foreign Policy 1918–1945 (DGFP), 7, 9, 13, 15–16, 19–24, 45, 48–50
Series D, Vol. X, *The War Years, June 23–August 31, 1940*, 22–3
Documents on Irish Foreign Policy, 63
Douglas-Home, Sir Alec. *See* Home, Earl of
Dublin, 9, 11–12, 23, 33, 44
Eden, Anthony, 6, 26
Einstein, Albert, 40
Eisenhower, President Dwight D., 22
Elizabeth the Queen Mother, Queen, 21

Elton, Geoffrey, 41

Ferris, John, 57

   Behind the Enigma: The Authorised History of GCHQ, 57

Financial Times, 59

First World War, 29–30, 37, 39

Foot, M.R.D., 52–53

   SOE in France, 52

   SOE in the Low Countries, 53

Foreign & Commonwealth Office (FCO). *See* Foreign Office (UK)

Foreign Ministry (Turkey), 64

Foreign Office (Germany), 6, 10, 19, 49–50

Foreign Office (UK) (FO, FCO), xi, 5–6, 9–10–11, 13–20, 26–9, 31–2, 38–40, 48–51, 53, 57–62, 65–7

   FCO Historians, 59–61

   Historical Branch, 57–59

   Historical Advisory Committee, 49–50

   Permanent Under-Secretary's Department (PUSD), 62

   minutes, publication of, 6, 13–15, 23, 29–30, 38–9, 48, 62, 67

Foreign Relations of the United States (FRUS), 61

Fox, Charles James, 1, 37n, 41

France, 7, 11, 18, 45n, 49, 64n

Frank Cass, 53

Frankfurt am Main, 19

Frankland, Noble, 36n, 46–7

   The Strategic Air Offensive against Germany (with Sir Charles Webster), 46–7

Frederick the Great, 37

Freedman, Sir Lawrence, 54

   The Falklands Campaign, 54

Freedom of Information Act, 57, 61

George VI, King, 22

Germany, vii–viii, 7

   Federal Republic, 22, 49–50, 59

   Nazi regime, 8n, 10, 17n, 40, 45n, 48

Weimar Republic, 49–50

Goebbels, Josef, 8n

Goltz, Rüdiger von der, 30

Gooch, G.P., 5, 7, 13–14, 29, 32, 59

Gourvish, Terry, 54

   The Channel Tunnel, 54

Gouzenko, Igor, 62

Gowing, Margaret, 5, 51

   Britain and Atomic Energy, 1939–1945, 51

   British War Economy (with Keith Hancock), 46

Grey, Sir Edward, 14

Grosse Politik der Europäischen Kabinette 1871–1914, Die, 5, 7, 11n, 25, 50, 63–4n

Gulf War (1991), 63

Gwynn, Father Aubrey, SJ, 17

Halifax, Viscount, 9, 12

Hamilton, Bill, 55–56

Hamilton, Keith, 50n, 59–60

Hancock (Sir) Keith (W.K.), 4–5, 43, 45–6, 51

   British War Economy (with Margaret Gowing), 46

Harris, Jose, 46

Harris, Sir Arthur, 47

Headlam-Morley, Sir James, 39

Healey, Lord (Denis), 54

Helsinki Conference (1975), 60

Hennessy, Lord (Peter), 55, 62

Her Majesty's Stationery Office (HMSO), 53

Hess, Rudolf, 59

Hinsley, (Sir) Harry, viii, 52

   British Intelligence in the Second World War, 52

History and Policy, 57

Hitler, Adolf, 8n, 11, 30, 48

Home Office, 57

Home, Earl of (Sir Alec Douglas-Home), 52, 58

House of Lords, 54–6

Howard, Sir Michael, 52
  Strategic Deception, 52
Howe, Sir Geoffrey (Lord), 54, 59
Hurd, Douglas, 59
Institut für Europäische Geschichte,
  Mainz, viii
International Committee of Historical
  Sciences, vii
International Conference of Editors of
  Diplomatic Documents (ICEDD),
  59, 63–4
International Military Tribunal,
  Nuremberg, 33
Iraq War, 63
Ireland, 1–2, 8, 12–13, 70
Italy, 63
Jeffery, Keith, 57
  MI6, 57
Joint Intelligence Committee, 62
Joll, James, 7
Kenya, 66
King's College London, 57
Know How Fund, 60
Koht, Halvdan, vii, 33
Krupp papers, 59
Lambert, Margaret, Hon, 22–3, 42–3
Lambert, Margaret. *See* Pelly, Margaret
  (née Lambert)
League of Nations, 35
Lexden, Lord, 55
Lisbon, 18
Listener, The, 1
London School of Economics (LSE), 36
Lower Saxony, 19
Macmillan, Harold, 47
Manchester Guardian, 2
Mansergh, Nicholas, 52
  The Transfer of Power, 1942–7, 52
Marburg, 7, 19
Marshall Plan (1948), 61
Marshall-Cornwall, Sir James, 7, 16n
Mau Mau campaign, 66
McIndoe, W.I., 51

Medlicott, Norton (W.N.), xi, 25–6,
  29–32, 36–8, 47, 49, 65
  The Economic Blockade, 25, 30
Mehta, Ved, 41–2
Meinecke, Friedrich, 10
Mercury, Perihelion of, 40
MI5, 65
Migrated archive, 66
Mile End Institute, 57
Milward, Alan, 54
  The Rise and Fall of a National
  Strategy 1945–1963, 54
Ministry of Defence, 53, 62
Ministry of Economic Warfare, 25, 30
Ministry of Information, 5, 13, 27
Morgan, D.J., 53
  The Official History of Colonial
  Development, 53
Morison, Stanley, 6
Munich Agreement (1938), 21, 30, 62
Mussolini, Benito, 30
Namier (Sir) Lewis, 1n, 7, 25, 45, 49
National Archives, The (TNA), 53, 61
Nazi–Soviet Relations 1939–1941, 10–13
Netherlands, 63
Newnham College, Cambridge 4
No. 10 Downing Street, 26, 62
Noack, Ulrich, 10
North Atlantic Treaty (1949), 61
Northern Ireland Department, 55
Norway
  alleged British invasion 1940, vii, 33
  German invasion 1940, vii, 33
O'Donnell, Sir Gus, 56
O'Sullivan, John, 17
Official Cabinet Office Committee on
  Official Histories (OH), 54
Official History of the Second World War
  Civil Series, 4, 45–6
  Military Series, 4, 45–7, 52–3
Official Secrets Act, 32, 65
Ording, Arne, 34
Oxford University Press, 52

Oxford, University of, 35–6n
Palmerston, Viscount, 14
Passant, James 9, 17, 20–2
Peacetime Official Histories, 51–7
Pelly, Margaret (née Lambert), 47, 58–9
Peterhouse, Cambridge, vii, 1, 4, 8–9,
    34–5, 41–2
Pilling, Sir Joe, 55–6
    Pilling report, 55–6
Poland, 45n, 63
Polish Diplomatic Documents, 63
Portal, Viscount, 47
Portugal, 18
Postan, Michael, 4
Potsdam Conference (1945), 62
Presnell, L.S.
    *External Economic Policy since the
    War*, 53
Princeton Institute for Advanced Study,
    1, 33, 42
ProQuest, 61
Public History Programme (proposed),
    55
Public Record Office (PRO), 31, 58–9
Public Records Act, 51
Queen Mary University of London, 57
Quisling, Vidkun, 10n
Raven, Charles, 17
Renouvin, Pierre, 11
Richards, Sir Brooks, 53
    Secret Flotillas, 53
Ritter, Gerhard, 10
Rodgers, Lord (Bill), 54–6
Routledge, 53, 61
Royal Family, 65
Royal Historical Society, 42–3
Russia, viii, 2, 12–13, 31, 37, 39–40. *See
    also* Soviet Union
Schmitt, Bernadotte E., 23
Second World War, 2, 5, 25, 28, 31, 37,
    39, 44, 52. *See also Official History
    of the Second World War*

Seldon, Sir Anthony, 63
Sidney Sussex College, Cambridge, 9
Simms, Brendan, 41
Smyth, Denis, vii
Society of Jesus, Irish Province of, 13
Sontag, Raymond J., 10–12, 21
South Africa, 43, 69, 73
Soviet Union, 7, 9, 12, 19, 40, 62, 70.
    See also Russia
Spain, 18
Spencer, Frank, 49
St John's College, Cambridge, viii
State Department (USA), 11–12, 19
Steiner, Zara, 59
Strand Group, 57
Strang, Sir William, 23
Studies: An Irish Quarterly Review, xi,
    13–14, 32
Suez crisis (1956), 52
Sweet, Paul W., 19–20, 24
Taylor & Francis, 53
Taylor, A.J.P., xi, 2–3, 6, 25, 27, 35, 40,
    45–6
    English History 1914–1945, 45–6, 62
Temperley, Harold, ix, xi, 3, 5–8, 13–14,
    26–7, 29, 32, 34–5, 41, 59
Thatcher, Margaret, 52, 61–2
    Margaret Thatcher Foundation,
    62n
thirty-year rule, 45, 51–2, 57–8, 60
Thuringia, 19
Times Literary Supplement (TLS), 2, 6
Titmuss, Richard, 46
    Problems of Social Policy, 46
Treasury, 57
Trevor-Roper, Hugh (Lord Dacre), 42n
Trinity Hall, Cambridge, 8n
Turkey, 64
twenty-year rule, 57
Ultra, 3, 52
United Kingdom Atomic Energy
    Authority, 51

United States of America (USA), 22, 39,
49–50, 72
University College Dublin (UCD),
vii, 3–4, 8, 12–13, 17–18, 33,
42
University College of Wales,
Aberystwyth, 59
Vansittart, Sir Robert, 10, 31, 38, 67
Vellacott, Paul, 8, 17, 34
Versailles, Treaty of (1919), 35
Vienna, Congress of (1814–15), 35
Vincent, John, 42
Waldegrave, William, 59
Watt, Donald Cameron, 50
Webster (Sir) Charles, 34–5, 46–7
*The Strategic Air Offensive
against Germany* (with Nobel
Frankland),46–7
Weizsäcker, Ernst von, 19
Welch, Colin, 8
Whaddon Hall, 7, 9, 11, 19–20
Wheatley, Ronald, 50
Wheeler-Bennett, (Sir) John, 7, 9, 11,
19, 21–2, 49
Whitehall History Publishing Group,
53, 56n
Whitehall, 55
Wiles Lectures, viii
Wilhelmstrasse. *See* Foreign Office
(Germany)
Williams, T. Desmond, ix–xi, 4,
8–13, 15–23, 32–3, 36, 42–4,
48–9
Wilson, Harold, 51–2
Wilson, Keith, 2
Windsor, Duchess of, 18
Windsor, Duke of, xi, 18–19
'Windsor papers', 18–23, 40, 66
Winterbotham, F.W., 52
The Ultra Secret, 52
Woodward (Sir) Llewellyn (E.L.), xi,
5–7, 10–12, 14, 16, 19–20, 25–32,
36n, 37–8, 42–3, 48–9, 61, 65

*British Foreign Policy in the Second
World War*, 28, 47
Yasamee, Heather, 59

INSTITUTE OF HISTORICAL RESEARCH | **SCHOOL OF ADVANCED STUDY** UNIVERSITY OF LONDON

The Institute of Historical Research (IHR) is the UK's national centre for history. Founded in 1921, the Institute facilitates and promotes innovative research via its primary collections library, and its programme of training, publishing, conferences, seminars and fellowships. The IHR is one of the nine humanities research institutes of the School of Advanced Study at the University of London.

'IHR Shorts' is a new Open Access publishing series from the Institute of Historical Research at the University of London. Insightful and concise, IHR Shorts offer incisive commentaries on contemporary historical debates. Titles typically range from 15,000 to 50,000 words with a focus on interdisciplinary approaches to the past.

1. Dethroning historical reputations: universities, museums and the commemoration of benefactors
edited by Jill Pellew and Lawrence Goldman (2018)

2. Magna Carta: history, context and influence
edited by Lawrence Goldman (2018)

3. Suffrage and citizenship in Ireland, 1912–18 (The Kehoe Lecture in Irish History 2018)
Senia Pašeta (2019)

4. European religious cultures: essays offered to Christopher Brooke on the occasion of his eightieth birthday
edited by Miri Rubin (2020)

CPSIA information can be obtained
at www.ICGtesting.com
Printed in the USA
LVHW070306160122
708351LV00002B/10

9 781914 477195